Come on Down!

A Little Story
About My Italian
Mom's Big Dream

Fran Tunno

At Fran's Table Media
Visit: www.AtFransTable.com
www.FranTunno.com

First Edition
Paperback ISBN: 979-8-9933682-0-7
eBook ISBN: 979-8-9933682-1-4

Contents

Preface

I started writing this book at the age of thirty-two, shelved it, then went back to it again and again. This book has dogged me through working, dating, marriage, kids, divorce, moving across the country (three times), parent caretaking and death, two job losses, a pandemic, and finally retirement. It's been a constant in the back of my mind and, like a pregnant woman way past her due date, I'm very ready to let it go.

When I started writing, I thought I was doing it because my stories of Mom could give others a laugh and some good recipes. With every rewrite I dug deeper and, in the process, learned it wasn't just those who'd never met my mother who needed this book, it was me. Writing these stories forced me to delve into my mom's life, and my strict Italian upbringing in the swinging '60s. Looking deeper helped me understand why growing up as I did embarrassed me, grounded me, and kept me a virgin much longer than the average 1970s college student. It gave me an appreciation for my mom's resilience, optimism, sense of humor, and her ability to laugh at herself. And it definitely increased my tremendous respect for my father's work ethic, humor, and incredibly gentle temperament.

She and my dad both taught me: It's not what life throws at you, it's how you respond that says everything about you. They responded with humor, love, hard work, patience, and food. This book is my thank-you to both my parents for being everything a child could want and more . . . even if they didn't make me go to bed at nine o'clock.

Introduction

In elementary school I yearned for a normal American mom, like June Cleaver of *Leave It to Beaver* fame. She wore pearls, had a waist, never raised her voice, roasted goat heads, cussed in Italian, or chased her kids around the house with a serving spoon. I never got that mom. But my stories and boxer-like reflexes are way better because of the mother life did give me.

I've tried to remember the details of my family's life, but hell, I'm seventy. Where the actual truth lies is a little squishy, so I've filled in the gaps as best I can with the help of parents, uncles, cousins, and siblings.

I could never write a book about Mom without including the thing she was best known for: force-feeding guests . . . not with a tube or anything, that would be gross. No, she'd just put the food in front of you, then watch you like a lion stalking prey until you ate an amount she found sufficient. Thankfully, she was a great cook and taught her kids everything she knew, so I've included a recipe, or two, or three, with each chapter. Some recipes are Mom's, some are mine, and some are my brothers'. Mom always said, "You gadda feed a da people!"

Fresh Peaches in Wine

Serves 1

Sip this while you read my book. It'll make me way more entertaining.

INGREDIENTS

1 fresh peach (yellow or white peaches are delicious, but canned peaches work)

1 glass of cabernet or merlot

STEPS

Peel the peach, cut it into chunks, and add them to the glass of wine. Stir and enjoy!

Come on Down!
A Little Story About
My Italian Mom's Big Dream

(Waiting Almost a Friggin' Lifetime for Her Fifteen Minutes of Fame)

J ohnny Olson's voice boomed, "Mary Tunno, come on down!" It was the moment my mom had dreamed of for a decade, and Johnny screwed it up by mispronouncing her name. He said, "Ton-oh" instead of "Toon-oh," the correct pronunciation. In Johnny's defense, his delivery was phonetically correct, but my mom was a rather large woman, so the visual was not ideal. If my mother noticed, she didn't show it.

"Meeeeee! Dey peeked a me!" my Italian American mother squealed as she jumped up from her seat beside me. Her smile filled her face. The camera followed her as she pumped her fists in triumph, gleefully trotting down the aisle while bouncy *Price Is Right* game show music played. Breathless, she arrived at Contestants' Row in a bright blue, short-sleeved dress that gently hugged her ample body.

Thank God, she got picked! I thought. *Finally, I can breathe* . . . until a new worry stuck its claws in my heart: *Oh God, what if she doesn't win something?*

My father, sitting to my left in the studio audience, leaned over and whispered in amazement, "I'll be damned, she said she'd get picked and she got picked!" For years she'd told Dad she believed she'd be a contestant on *The Price Is Right*, and there we were, on June 21, 1982, witnessing that belief become reality.

While aspiring to be a game show contestant might not be a big stretch for the average person, it was huge for my mom. With her second-grade education, Italian accent, and Cinderella beginnings, most of her small-town friends just silently shook their heads when she brought it up.

After almost a decade of hoping and waiting, my dad and I watched from one of the back rows of Studio 33 at CBS Television City in Los Angeles as my mom finally met her idol, game show host, Bob Barker, under the glare of studio lights.

Dad and I sat stunned as Mom worked her magic. Reaching her assigned spot, she captivated the entire audience with her childlike exuberance. The first, almost tearful words out of her mouth were, "I been wanting to see you for a long a time!" The audience responded with a collective "Aww!" Bob stood onstage and teasingly said, "Well Mary, all you had to do was turn on your television." Mom was completely charmed as her idol asked, "Where do you live?"

She forgot almost everything about herself in her nervousness, only remembering that she was from Pennsylvania. Bob said, "Oh, so you're out here on vacation," which was enough to snap her back. She became very animated and then, as if she'd rehearsed it a million times, said, "Well yes, I came a because a my daughter, she says a 'Ma, you wanna see Bob a Barker? I'mma gonna move to California and you getta to come here.'"

I heard those words and thought, *Oh God, I'm slipping . . . I'm embarrassed again. Now it's not just regular small-town embarrassment, it's nationally televised embarrassment.* Mom's words were an almost entirely fabricated twist on what really happened, and Bob wasn't buying it for a second. But my mother was a born storyteller, apparently determined to convince the world that I was the patron saint of game show wannabes.

Why Mom felt she needed to win and why she chose a game show host as her vehicle for infatuation, fame, and fortune, are questions only she could answer. And I'm sure she had her reason for telling the entire world that I quit my job and moved 2,500 miles away so she could be on *The Price Is Right*, but I have my theories.

I think Bob reignited a spark lit in Mom when she was in her twenties and told she looked like Pola Negri, a Polish film star. They shared a beautiful broad face, black hair, and expressive eyes. When she sat in darkened movie theaters in the 1930s, she could imagine she was that star on the screen. For that golden ninety minutes every few weeks she could forget she was her tavern-owning parents' least favorite child, in her twenties, still unmarried, and living under their roof . . . and thumb. Movies were her favorite escape from hours working as her parents' tavern barmaid for no pay and fueled secret dreams of being that starlet.

Decades later, and married with four kids, *The Price Is Right* became her last chance to grab that fast-evaporating sliver of Hollywood fame. After a lifetime of being an obedient daughter, then a good wife and mother, she could now, without a doubt, prove to the world *she* was the star.

She felt she had a chance on *The Price Is Right*, where everyday people could win via a combination of knowledge and luck. One woman in her 500-card club scoffed at my mother's chances saying, "And what makes you think *you* have a chance?" which thoroughly inflamed Mom's finely honed revenge gene. It was another person not believing in her and made her even more determined to get on that show and win.

As for her attempt at getting me into the annals of sainthood, maybe she thought she could make me famous. As we all know, producers and directors frequently watch game shows hoping to find their next Meryl Streep.

Mom could only dream of being on *The Price Is Right* after it first aired in 1972 because my bricklayer father did not share her enthusiasm for Mr. Barker. He said all Hollywood celebrities could go jump in a lake for all he cared, so Dad was not spending his hard-earned money to fly to LA and do the game show circuit. Mom's children were all grown. I was in college and the others were working, two with families of their own, so they weren't going to take her either. And she was too afraid to go alone.

So she passed her time in the '70s watching *The Price Is Right* on the portable TV in her western Pennsylvania dining room. Every weekday at 11:00 a.m. she guessed along with the contestants, dreaming of the day she'd join them. Interruptions were not well-tolerated. If any of us walked in while the show was on and tried to talk to her, she held up her hand and said, "Wait, I'mma watchin' da *Price Issa Right!*" My father called it the holy hour.

The rest of her day was spent cooking, canning, force-feeding anyone who dropped by, doing laundry, ironing clothes, scratching off lottery tickets (with all her fingers crossed—try it, it's not easy), cleaning, praying for grandchildren—males first, of course (more on that later), and plotting how soon she could get her (hopefully virgin) daughters married.

She resigned herself to thinking that if there wasn't a chance at getting her moment of fame on national television, then she'd continue doing her best to make sure her offspring made something of themselves—that would be almost as good. Years went by like that until that day in June 1982 when everything changed because of me.

She was finally going to prove, to her long-dead parents, who never valued her, and anyone else who dared doubt her, that she was extraordinary. But first, she'd have to win. And the road from our home in New

Brighton, Pennsylvania, to Television City would include delays, detours, heartbreak, child-rearing, embarrassment, contests, spatula-wielding chase scenes, Italian curse words, a lot of food, intense scrutiny of potential spouses, and the holy Catholic Apostolic Church.

Fran's "Italian American" Pasta Sauce
Serves 10 to 12

Sunday sauce is a must for Italian families and a great dish for celebrating getting on a game show. I loved my mom and learned all I know from her, but her sauce was not my favorite . . . I'm waiting for the lightning bolt. Anyway, this sauce is hers with a few tweaks. I'm also including the recipe for my uncle Richard's famous meatballs.

INGREDIENTS

1 whole head of garlic (about 12 cloves), separated, peeled, and crushed or minced

2 tablespoons olive oil

2 tablespoons butter

5 to 6 meaty pork ribs with bones

6 mild Italian sausages

5 (28 ounces) or 2 (90 ounces) cans Cento Italian Whole Peeled Tomatoes (The added basil makes them taste as close as you can get to my mom's homemade canned tomatoes, which were godly.)

1 (6 ounces) can tomato paste

2 tablespoons dry Italian seasoning

2 tablespoons chopped fresh basil

¾ teaspoon fresh rosemary

1 tablespoon fresh parsley

½ cup cabernet or merlot

¼ cup apple juice concentrate (optional, for sweetener)

Salt and pepper

STEPS

1. In a large, deep pot over medium-low heat, add the garlic, oil, and butter. Brown the pork and sausage—taking care not to burn the garlic. (Turn off the heat while processing the tomatoes or it might burn.)

2. Remove the tomatoes from the cans and cut each in half; remove the seeds. Place them in a large blender or food processor for a few seconds, until just blended.

3. Pour the tomatoes over the meats and garlic and cook over low heat, stirring well to combine. Add the tomato paste, Italian seasoning, basil, rosemary, and parsley. Add the wine and taste; if it needs sweetening, add the apple juice concentrate—it's optional. Add salt and pepper to taste.

4. Place a heat diffuser under the pot to avoid burning. Cook the sauce for 3 hours, stirring every 20 minutes or so, until the meat is falling off the bone.

5. Serve over pasta with grated Parmigiano, Romano, or Pecorino, and enjoy!

Uncle Richard's Famous Meatballs

Makes 22 to 25

Even Mom knew his meatballs were better than hers. She didn't like to admit it, though. Anyway, you can make sauce with meatballs instead of the sausage, but the best sauce always has a few pork ribs in it, so don't forget those. Add these meatballs to your sauce and let them cook about an hour.

Addendum: This was the recipe Uncle Richard shared with me. But, his daughter, Nancy, says Uncle Richard changed his recipes all the time. She says he often used one pound of ground beef, a half-pound of pork and a half-pound of veal, which she thinks tastes best. But he altered his recipes depending on what was in the refrigerator. (Italians and their recipes! Sheesh!)

INGREDIENTS

⅓ cup fresh basil, finely chopped

¼ cup finely chopped fresh parsley

4 cloves of garlic, minced

¾ teaspoon finely chopped fresh rosemary

2 slices of white bread, soaked in water or milk, then squeezed

1½ pounds ground beef

1½ pounds ground pork

2 mild Italian sausage links

1 teaspoon Worcestershire sauce

1 teaspoon hot sauce (optional)

¾ teaspoon pepper

1 tablespoon salt

¾ cup Italian-style breadcrumbs

¼ cup grated Parmigiano or Romano

2 eggs

8 ounces red wine for dipping the meatballs in

1 ½ cups flour for rolling the meatballs in

3 cups vegetable oil (canola or olive) for frying

STEPS

1. Place the basil, parsley, garlic, and rosemary into a food processor. Then add the soaked, drained bread and process until it's all combined.

2. Mix the three meats and add the processed bread-and-herb mixture in a bowl. Then add the Worcestershire sauce, hot sauce, pepper, salt, breadcrumbs, cheese, and eggs.

3. Mix thoroughly with your hands. Take a small piece and fry it in some oil in a frying pan. Taste it and see what it needs. We discovered it might need a little more salt when we did ours. (Uncle Richard and I tested this, of course . . . but this is all to taste, so you can decide.)

4. Roll the mixture into two-inch balls, first in the red wine, then in the flour.

5. Fry the meatballs until browned on all sides; then add them to your tomato sauce. Cook for about an hour, then serve with the pasta of your choice.

The Plans

Plan A for the average aspiring star would be to move out of your parents' house, head to Hollywood, take acting classes, be amazing, get discovered, then become famous! But Plan A didn't have an ice cube's chance in hell of happening.

Mom's very strict parents would have prohibited her from leaving and she never dared disobey them. Plus, she didn't drive, had no car, and no money to leave. My mother taking acting classes would have been amusing for the other actors because if a fellow thespian had dared try to kiss her, she would have walloped him. Her mother drilled into her head that only *puttànas* (whores) go further than hand-holding, even if it is only acting.

Knowing Plan A was impossible, my mom could have just given up completely—that would have been Plan B. Of course, Plan B was never going to happen either because she stubbornly held on to the feeling deep inside that she was someone and deserved to be valued, even if her parents didn't realize it.

Plan C was the route she took. It included obeying her parents, getting married, having children, entering every contest available (legal and illegal), and making sure her kids grew up to be well-behaved, healthy, and did their best. Their successes would be her success, and that might have to be enough.

Fran's Fork-Tender Stuffed Pork Chops
Serves 6

If you're going to run off and be a star, you better eat something substantial to get you there!

INGREDIENTS

1 package of pork-flavored Stove Top Stuffing Mix (I know it's prepackaged; get over it, it's good.)

¾ cup dried cranberries

1 cup celery, chopped into ¾-inch pieces

3 medium to large apples, cut into ½-inch slices (any kind will work, but I use Granny Smith)

3 medium to large brown onions, cut into ½-inch slices

6 thick boneless pork chops (about 1½ inches thick so you can stuff them)

Meat tenderizer

½ cup Progresso Bread Crumbs Italian Style

6 strips (or more) of bacon

1 cup baby carrots

STEPS

1. Preheat the oven to 350°F. Spray a large baking pan or deep glass dish (9 x 11-inch or larger) with nonstick spray.

2. In a medium saucepan, prepare the package of Stove Top according to directions. Add the dried cranberries and celery to the prepared stuffing, mixing thoroughly. Place a lid on the saucepan and set it aside.

3. Place the sliced apples into the large baking pan. Add the onions and mix thoroughly, allowing the onion slices to fall apart.

4. Slice the pork chops along one side, creating a pocket so you can place the stuffing inside. Sprinkle each chop lightly with tenderizer inside and out. Stuff 2 to 4 tablespoons of stuffing inside each pocket. When full, lightly press it together and lay the chop on top of the apple-onion mixture. Repeat with each chop. (Serve any extra stuffing on the side.)

5. Lightly sprinkle the top of the pork chops with the breadcrumbs (it keeps them moist).

6. Cut the bacon slices in half, and place them on top of the stuffed, sprinkled chops. (The bacon fat drips onto the chops, keeping them moist and adding more flavor, and oh baby, are they good!)

7. Arrange the carrots around the pork chops.

8. Cover the pan tightly with aluminum foil and bake for 3 to 3.5 hours. Chops should be golden brown and fork-tender. You can remove the bacon when the chops are done and place it underneath the chop when serving, because who doesn't love bacon?

If Your Mother Is Convinced You're Great, Who Are You to Argue?

(1958)

Advertising in the 1950s and '60s in America was filled with images of adorable little girls with baby-doll faces, blond hair, and big blue eyes. They graced everything from Northern toilet paper to Coppertone suntan lotion. I was not one of them.

Look no further than this May 1958 photograph. My sister, Mary, had just made her first Communion. My parents captured the day with photos of my sister in her Communion finery on the front lawn. Mary is on the right in her lacy white dress. I'm the three-year-old vagbond with Medusa-like hair on the left.

My mother never acknowledged any shortcomings. She told me and my siblings we could do anything. She constantly reminded me I was the cutest, smartest, best kid around, and was really going to be something someday.

Yeah, she was probably delusional. But she was determined to make me and my siblings do our best. It all stemmed from the fact that my mom, Mary Louise Carcaise, had the misfortune of being her Italian immigrant parents' least favorite child.

Although Mary was my grandparents' first child born in the United States of America, even going to the trouble to be born on the Fourth of July in 1913, apparently Giulia and Giovanni Carcaise (formerly Carcaiso) were not impressed. Nevertheless, my mom relished her American citizenship status, as if the founding fathers had simultaneously risen from the dead and painstakingly planned it.

There are two versions of Mary's early life: one official, one spicy. The ho-hum official story went that shortly after my mom was born, my grandmother missed her loving family *so* much, and her relatives were *so* anxious to meet the new baby, she took my infant mother and my one-year-old aunt to her hometown of Sparanise, Italy, to get acquainted . . .

Sorry, I dozed off. If you're still awake, here's the slightly spicier version that explains my grandparents' lack of matrimonial zeal:

Giulia got fed up and left Giovanni because she wanted a nicer home and he had a wandering eye . . . possibly two of them. I'm not sure how she made her escape, because this had to have taken some planning, but Giovanni must have come home and discovered his wife had packed up their daughters and was gone. A move this drastic makes it pretty clear that more than just eyes must have been wandering.

Maybe Giulia knew she was pregnant when she left with her two daughters, maybe not. But either way, in 1913, a woman wouldn't just take off alone with an infant, a toddler, and morning sickness, on a two-week boat journey across the Atlantic, without a good reason. I have to give her credit; that was gutsy.

World War I broke out on July 28, 1914, and lasted four years, so coming back during the war was too dangerous. That was followed by the 1918 pandemic that lasted until 1920. My grandparents were probably thrilled the world was in turmoil because at least they had an excuse for not reuniting.

Giovanni definitely took his time, but in 1925, twelve years after my grandmother's escape, he finally dragged himself to Sparanise and retrieved his wife and three daughters: Jenny, Mary, and Johanna, who were now thirteen, twelve, and eleven, and brought them back to Rochester, Pennsylvania, where Mary had made her initial firecracker entrance.

The photo on this page is Mary outside her new home in Rochester at about twelve years old. The father she was just getting to know already had a nickname for her. It was *mat-sud*, which was his crude Neapolitan slang meaning "big ass." He was clearly not a contender for Father of the Year. Yet Mary defended him, always saying he was just kidding.

Giovanni and Giulia deposited their three daughters at nearby Saint Cecilia Catholic School, where the clueless nuns stuck them in second grade. Mary said the teacher wrote a math problem on the chalkboard one day and she blurted out the answer, *"Ventiquattro!"* in Italian. All the pipsqueak seven-year-olds laughed at her and she was mortified. She had learned the basics in school in Italy, like printing, writing, and counting, but her education didn't go very far. Girls were encouraged to crochet, embroider, and cook, so they could become good wives, not CEOs.

School was awful and her long-absent father wasn't filling her with confidence. Mary's mother knew she'd be helpful raising the kids and cleaning the house, so Mary quit school, stayed home, scrubbed, changed diapers, cooked, cleaned, and was still not valued.

She did have a grandmother who shared her name, lived with the family, and loved her, but she passed away when Mary was fourteen. It's like a sad 1930s Italian Cinderella tale, without perky woodland animals showing up to serenade her while industriously scrubbing the floors and designing her clothes. Even though the adversity stunk, Mary leaned into it and learned a hard lesson.

Peanut Butter and Apricot Jam Roll-ups
Makes 10 (1-inch) rolls

Mom made these from leftover pie-crust scraps. We LOVED them! They make every child feel special. You can use a store-bought pie crust, but of course my mom's recipe is best.

Mary Tunno's Pie Crust
Makes about 3 to 4 (9-inch) pie crusts

INGREDIENTS
2½ cups flour

1 teaspoon salt

1 tablespoon sugar

1 cup butter, cut into ½-inch pieces

½ cup (or more) ice-cold whole milk

For the roll-ups:

½ to ¾ cup peanut butter (Laura Scudder's or Costco, or any natural smooth peanut butter; you may need to warm it slightly if it's too hard to spread easily)

⅓ to ½ cup apricot preserves

STEPS

1. Preheat the oven to 350°F.

2. Combine the flour, salt, and sugar in a food processor. Add the butter and process until it looks like medium-sized crumbs. Add the milk and pulse until it just comes together.

3. Dump the dough on a lightly floured countertop and squeeze together. Roll it out until about 1 inch thick, cut in half, and put one piece on top of the other.

4. Then roll that out to about 1 inch thickness and cut it again; place one piece on top of the other.

5. Press the layers together and roll it out slightly. Cut into four pieces, wrap each in cellophane, and chill them until ready to make your pie. Or freeze them until you are ready to use them at a later date. (Be careful if you defrost them in the microwave because they defrost in seconds!)

6. Roll out one piece of dough on a lightly floured surface to about a ¼ inch thickness. Spread the crust evenly with the peanut butter, then the apricot preserves over the peanut butter, leaving about a ½-inch border uncovered around the edges.

7. Roll up the dough covered with peanut butter and jam into a log. Moisten the edges with a tiny bit of water so they stick together and no jam leaks out. (Some may leak out anyway.)

8. Place the roll on a cookie sheet and bake for 20 to 30 minutes, or until golden brown.

9. Let the roll cool and cut into 1-inch pieces.

Two Cinderellas Meet

Both my parents had miserable teen years, but the award for worst timing in adolescence goes to my dad.

My grandfather Bernardo was desperate to escape Italy's oppressive poverty in the early 1900s and make a better life for his family in the United States. How poor were they? My father said he was so hungry once that he grabbed a rock and smashed in the head of one of the family's chickens so they could have meat for dinner. When his mother asked what had happened to it, he shrugged, but was secretly thrilled he would get to eat chicken that night.

My grandfather did everything right. He learned English, came to the US legally, worked here for five years, leaving his wife and kids behind, and was finally granted citizenship in 1928. You'd think that would have created some kind of good karma for him. You'd be wrong.

He planned to bring the family over a little at a time because it was too expensive to bring them all at once, so he started with his oldest sons, my dad, Ubaldo, who was fourteen, and my uncle Fred, who was seventeen.

In August 1929 they arrived in Monaca, Pennsylvania, which is just across the river from Rochester, where Mary lived. My grandfather and his two sons stayed with family friends. Their plan was to work and make money. God had a pretty good chuckle over that.

Ubaldo's fourteenth birthday was October 24, 1929. It's also known as Black Thursday in the US because it's the day the stock market started its disastrous decline, finally crashing on October 29. Then came the Depression. So much for making money . . . or karma.

Fred got a job at the glass factory, my dad was going to school, and my grandfather had to take any job he could find. They were boarders at their friend's home, and things were very tight. The family they were staying with had three children of their own, and they took in two additional boarders to make ends meet. Ubaldo and Ferdinando (Fred) slept in beds at night but had to get up at 6:00 a.m. because they shared those beds with the two boarders who worked the night shift. When Ubaldo wanted to take a bath, he said he had to bathe in the river and wasn't allowed to eat at the dining table with the family.

Ubaldo attended school but, like my mom, didn't speak English. His teacher stayed after class to help him, and he made up his mind to learn English and speak it without an accent. The teacher changed his name from Ubaldo to Robert so it would be easier for others to pronounce.

Robert was miserable and completely homesick, so his father scraped together enough for a round-trip ticket to Italy. Robert happily went back, staying for two years. But his father made him return because he wasn't about to waste the other half of a perfectly good round-trip ticket. Decades later, Robert still remembered his mother tearfully running after the train as it pulled away.

Once back in the States, Robert was thrilled to join the Civilian Conservation Corps. It paid him thirty dollars a month and transported him around the country to do manual labor that he loved. But when his CCC days were over, he was back living in the same house in Monaca and hopeless again. A good friend asked him to be the best man in his wedding and that's where Robert met Mary, who was the maid of honor.

The two Cinderellas went on a few dates and found out they were in situations each of them despised. He visited her at her parents' tavern and wanted to help her leave the job she hated. She learned he was living as a boarder in a home where he didn't feel like he belonged. After only three months, they took the plunge into marriage.

Robert said, "I really didn't know her well, but she was quiet and pretty, so I hoped it would work out." Mary said, "I looked at his hands and saw they were calloused, so I knew he was a hard worker. He was handsome, nice, and had respect, so I knew he was a good man."

It wasn't love at first sight, or a racing-heart kind of romance. It was built on mutual respect, practicality, and a little despera-tion, because they both wanted out of where they were.

Mary was twenty-seven years old and considered an old maid in 1940. Her father, who walked his other daughters down the aisle, refused to walk with Mary. God only knows why, but she was walked down the aisle by a cousin.

While Mary and Robert were posing for wedding photos, Mary said she heard her late grandmother saying, "Smile, Mary, you have every-thing to smile about." Mary did seem to have a bit of a sixth sense, so maybe her grandmother really did peer into the future and was sending Mary the message that she would finally get the love she deserved.

As they started building a life and home together, Mary learned that Robert took work very seriously and was every bit as nice as she'd thought. Robert learned that Mary was a little rougher around the edges than he'd anticipated. But it didn't stop them from staying together and molding their children into small, hardworking hunter-gatherers who would do their best to make their parents proud.

Robert's Polenta

Makes 6 servings

This was the only dish Robert ever made (except for his Christmas Eels, which out of respect for you, will not be featured in this book). He cooked polenta on really cold days, and Mary served it with tomato sauce, sausage, and cheese. Robert's family in Italy was very poor, and this was one thing they could afford to eat. You can serve it with my "Italian American" Pasta Sauce.

INGREDIENTS

5 cups water or chicken or vegetable broth (broth gives it more flavor)

¼ teaspoon (or more) salt (if not using broth)

¾ cup cornmeal or polenta meal (make sure your cornmeal is fresh—it can get rancid and taste bitter if it's too old)

¼ cup grated Parmigiano or Romano cheese

3 tbsp. butter

STEPS

1. Bring the water to a boil in a medium to large pot; add the salt and stir.

2. Slowly pour in the cornmeal, stirring with a whisk constantly. Cook over medium heat until the mixture thickens and the cornmeal is soft (20 minutes to 45 minutes).

3. When thickened, stir in the cheese and the butter.

4. Ladle the polenta into a bowl, top with Fran's Italian American Pasta sauce and sausage, and sprinkle with Pecorino Romano cheese. Serve hot.

That Whole Greatness Thing?
You Start Buying into It

Mary's parents' lack of love for her left her heartsick but determined to prove to them and everyone else that she was someone. Once she got married, that extended to us, her children. Anything we achieved was proof something good could come from her, so we all got the "Be the Best" speech. Even though I looked like a frizzy, disheveled Italian Little Debbie, my mom did her best to convince me greatness was ahead. I wasn't so sure.

Early childhood was pretty good. My siblings were reasonably kind. My brothers shared a bedroom like my sister and I. Bernie, who was twelve years my senior, was kind. He always took time to play with me and sometimes even bought me cute clothes. Bob, who was nine years older, occasionally played with me but mostly ignored me. My sister, Mary, who was four and a half years older, and very strong, sometimes played with me but also threatened me nightly if I didn't do her bidding during the day, or if I laughed when my brothers teased her, which happened frequently. These were dangerous times, but personal appearance and death threats aside, things were OK from zero to five.

Serious realization came when I started public school kindergarten and discovered that being "the best" is based on something ridiculous called a report card. So I started creating fictional tales to compensate for my average progress.

One day, after school, I walked through our side door and up the three yellow linoleum steps into our 1950s kitchen. My mom was working at the sink when I proudly announced, "Ma, I was so good today, the teacher made everyone else go back to class and let only me play on the playground extra-long!"

I don't know how I came up with that stroke of genius. It wasn't planned, it just came out because I knew she wanted to be proud of me.

My mom totally bought it, but my sister saw right through it, accusing me of lying later when we were alone. "That didn't really happen, did it?" she said menacingly. "Yes, it did!" I backed up my fiction with another good solid lie. There's a lifetime of therapy ahead for a kid who makes up stories like that.

First grade was the start of Catholic school at Saint Joseph's Elementary in New Brighton, which quashed my blossoming career as a creative liar. My mom and I filed through Saint Joseph's heavy front doors, past the cafeteria, and up worn concrete stairs to my first-grade classroom. My teacher, a nun in long black robes, stood waiting for us on the gleaming hardwood floors in sensible black-laced leather shoes.

After our introductions, my mom proudly stood beside me and said, "Sister, listen, iffa Francy doesn't behave, you give her a good a smack. She'll listen!"

I remember looking at her and thinking, *Dear God, Ma, are you nuts?*

This nun looks dangerous! How can you betray me like this? First grade was a time of other unpleasant surprises too. I discovered:

1. I was not the cutest, smartest, or best.
2. My mom was unlike any other mother, and very possibly a medieval time traveler.
3. Great storytelling was referred to as lying and, worse yet, it was a sin that would take me straight to hell, or if I was lucky, Purgatory.
4. Everyone was clearly not Italian because the cafeteria's macaroni with tomatoes and beef was an abomination
5. My hair was going to need some attention.

Becoming the best was starting to look very iffy. Then dark reality struck with Saint Joseph's Elementary School Christmas play. Nun casting for the play proved I was clearly not the best because a first-grade classmate was chosen to be the star, portraying a cute toy doll sitting in Santa's lap. She wore a beautiful light-blue dress with a big bow in the back, a puffy, starched petticoat, and got to say, "Mama."

That was when I began to suspect that cute girls with blue eyes, straight hair, and pretty clothes got more attention than those of us with fuzzy brown hair, brown eyes and three dresses for the school year. Not that I'm still bitter or anything.

I was forced to make my Christmas debut as a lifeless nurse doll. What was I thinking, asking for that nurse's outfit in the Spiegel catalog? As soon as the nuns got wind of it, I was typecast.

I tried to embrace my role. I sat onstage, surrounded by other child "dolls." We leaned against each other, trying to look as glassy-eyed and lifeless as possible. But, in my white cap and dress with navy-blue cape and Red Cross emblem, I looked more like a small dead nurse.

In second grade, the nuns decided that since I'd done such an outstanding job as a lifeless nurse doll in first grade, I should do a repeat performance. From third through fifth grade my enthusiasm for the Christmas play evaporated as I morphed from dead nurse to invisible member of the chorus.

Finally, in sixth grade I got my big break as one of the snowflake dancers—the juicy role my mother knew I was destined for. This would prove her right. I'd be a star!

There were four girls and four boys in our group. The nuns even brought in Ruthie Helble, the local tap dance teacher to teach us step, shuffle, hop, so we could wow the crowd with our dance moves.

Each week through November and December we trudged across the cracked blacktop of the playground, past fading yellow dodgeball circles and down concrete steps into the silent church basement. We practiced while the Sisters of Saint Joseph transformed plywood backdrops into snow-covered hills and magical toy lands.

On the big night, folding wooden chairs were lined up in anticipation of a packed house. Our Christmas shows started with the first-grade class and ended with the eighth-grade class's grand finale, the nativity scene. Any girl with long brown hair got to be Mary, and any boy with facial hair got to be Joseph. Baby Jesus was played by someone's Hedda Get Bedda doll wrapped in swaddling clothes.

Powdered and rouged to simulate scarlet fever, we waited backstage until the class before us was done. We filed onto the stage, in formation, in white turtlenecks and red skirts and pants. I held the sweaty hand of my partner, Jerry Leahy, and started off with a step, shuffle, hop.

The creaky plywood stage swayed with every hop, but we were dancing! Until some of us stepped when we should have hopped. We stood there looking at each other like shell-shocked sheep. I kept imagining the disappointment of the nuns and our parents.

Everything was hopelessly ruined, and Jerry, the boy with the worst temper in class, was making matters worse by scowling on stage. Even then I knew the show must go on, so I smiled sweetly at the audience, hoping my joie de vivre would distract them from my lumberjack dance moves. Then, like a Mafia boss, I whispered in Jerry's ear, "Smile or I'll break your neck." The shock planted a tiny smile on his face.

I looked up, flushed from embarrassment and six pounds of rouge, scanning the darkness of the packed-in audience. I spotted her in seconds. First, the silver cat's-eye glasses reflecting the light, then the wavy black hair, the ample body, and the widest smile in the crowd. There was no missing my mother. As soon as she'd caught my eye, she pointed me out proudly, and loudly, to everyone around her.

There I was, making threats and shuffling out of step, and my mom only saw the star she believed I was. She stood out like the pulsing neon of Las Vegas in the black desert night, literally ready to burst out of her seat and explode with pride. My mother had no idea what being reserved meant when it came to her children—even ones screwing up the snowflake dance. (I'm happy to report that we nailed the dance the next night.) The knot I felt in my stomach was happiness mixed with embarrassment over her exuberance.

That image of my mom beaming at me at the Christmas play is my most cherished childhood memory. She'd convinced herself I was already amazing and was really going to be something someday, so who was I to argue? Maybe there was hope for me. She simply wouldn't offer anything but encouragement because she remembered too well how hurtful it was when she'd hoped for support from her father and got quite the opposite.

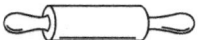

Mom's Glove Cookies
(*I Guanti*, or as Mom would say, "E Wandy")
Makes approximately 25 to 35

My mom may have been devoted, but she was no fool. Throughout my elementary school years she sent a big plate of bribery cookies to the nuns at Christmas. They included sugary, lemony fried twists called *I Guanti* (gloves). The number of cookies depends on how large you make each cookie.

These cookies are delicious fried bites of dough, lightly crisp on the outside but tender inside, with lemon, orange, and vanilla flavors. I did graduate from eighth grade, so apparently they did the trick. (Mom's original recipe made enough to sway the entire school district, so I cut it in thirds for you.)

The dough can also be used to make *struffoli*, or fried dough with honey and nuts. It's enough that you can use three-quarters of the dough for the Glove cookies and one-quarter for the *struffoli* recipe.

INGREDIENTS

4 cups flour

1 tablespoon baking powder

⅛ teaspoon baking soda

1 ¼ cups sugar

⅛ teaspoon salt

5 teaspoons milk

5½ eggs

1 tablespoon olive oil

⅛ cup Butter Flavor Crisco

2 teaspoons vanilla

1 teaspoon lemon juice

1 lemon rind

¼ orange rind

4 teaspoons whiskey

⅛ teaspoon anise extract

1 to 2 cups granulated sugar for sprinkling

1 quart vegetable oil for frying

STEPS

1. In a medium bowl, mix the flour, baking powder, baking soda, sugar, and salt.

2. In a separate bowl, mix the eggs, olive oil, Crisco, vanilla, lemon juice, citrus rinds, whiskey, and anise extract.

3. Add the dry ingredients to the liquid ingredients to form a soft dough.

4. Roll out the dough ¼ inch thick on a floured board, and cut it into long strips.

5. Separate each strip and fold it over, like a pretzel, then deep-fry in hot vegetable oil until golden brown.

6. When the cookies are done, spread them in a large container and immediately sprinkle them with sugar.

For the struffoli:

1. Just roll the same dough into long, thin rolls about ½ inch wide, and cut the rolled dough into one-inch bits, or smaller.

2. Deep-fry the dough bits until golden brown. You should have at least 3 cups.

3. Add ⅓ cup, or more, of toasted whole hazelnuts.

4. Then boil 1 cup of honey, and pour it over the fried dough bits and nuts, mixing them so they're all covered in honey. Be careful: Hot honey burns!

5. Arrange the *struffoli* in a circle (like a doughnut) and let them cool; then sprinkle them with nonpareils and serve.

Parents Can Make or Break You

The road to success can be a slog. My parents had different approaches. My father believed hard work and discipline led to success. My mother felt hard work and discipline were important, but she learned from experience that you have to build confidence in children by always supporting them. Most people gain confidence by putting themselves out there and showing some special talent. Everyone oohs and aahs. The adulation builds assurance, and next, you're starring in a Hollywood movie or running the free world.

My oldest brother, Bernie, was good at sports, a fabulous accordion player, and could make friends with anyone. My other brother, Bob, was studious, brainy, strong, and disciplined, which was good, because his accordion teacher said, "I die a little bit every time you play." My sister, Mary, was artistic, creative, and good at hair, makeup, and threatening looks. She could go into cosmetology or become an assassin. And I was clearly not going to be a dancer but was good at being a ham and a smart-ass.

Ham and smart-ass weren't sought-after skill sets in the 1960s, so my prospects were dubious. But Mom never stopped cheering me on because of an experience with her father, decades earlier.

Sometime in the warm months of 1937 she attended the Rochester Community Picnic sponsored by the Rochester Businessmen's Association. The picnic included a short river cruise. As the boat slowly made its way along the Ohio River, a beauty contest was announced for the best-looking blonde and brunette. (Back then, men were always holding beauty contests just for the joy of openly ogling women.)

My mother was a black-haired beauty, twenty-four years old, with rich, chocolate-brown eyes and a nice figure. A young man in the crowd kept winking at her and urging her to enter for best looking brunette. She was used to men paying attention to her and knew a lot of them because they ate and drank at her parents' tavern.

Giovanni and Giulia knew men would come in to see her because she was pretty and cost them nothing, so she was the perfect employee. Plus, she looked great on their annual Christmas greeting card.

"You're prettier than any of them, Mary—go on," the young man urged. She was embarrassed and didn't want to go, but he kept pestering her, so she mustered up her courage and headed toward the stage. As she passed by her father in the audience, he said, "If you go up there, I don't know you."

More than fifty years later she tearfully recounted, in the Italian accent she never lost, that his remark still stung. "After hearing hissa words, I stood onstage and wished dare was a hole I could jump into, I felt so ashamed."

But when they announced she was the winner of the contest for prettiest brunette, she said it felt like someone had lifted an enormous weight from her heart. She looked out in the crowd and saw her father standing there, smiling after her victory, and felt a flood of relief.

That day cemented my mom's decision that she'd never treat her children like she was treated. My grandfather's lack of encouragement left my mom determined to be our most vocal cheerleader, even through bad dance performances.

Her victory on that boat also gave her the courage to compete again and again, winning local beauty contests and the Miss Beaver County title.

That makes me the daughter of Miss Beaver County, a title I was always proud of until my teen years when I heard my aunt Blanche talking about some woman's beaver. I was confused because I didn't think people kept beavers as pets, even in Beaver County.

Then I discovered that *beaver* has another, less prestigious connotation meaning a woman's lady parts. Here's a colorful verbatim definition of the word *beaver* I found on Google: *The term originated several hundred years ago when the prostitutes wore beaver pelts to cover their genitalia due to a need to shave and prevent an infestation of lice in their pubic hair*

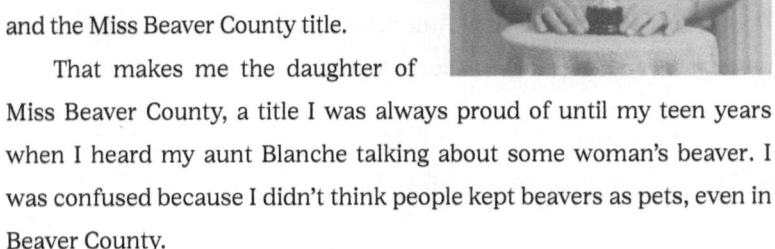

as a result of a serious lice epidemic. Ever feel a beaver pelt? The beaver's fur is very soft.

See? And you thought you weren't going to learn anything from this book! Now that I'm older and slightly wiser, I'm proud to be the daughter of Miss Beaver County, because winning that title wasn't just about being pretty; winning finally gave my mom a feeling of worth.

It's why tears streamed down her face when she watched the *Miss America Pageant* and *Queen for a Day*, shows I always thought were ridiculous and hokey. I understand now, that every time she saw a crown placed on a girl's head, she was reliving her moment of finally feeling good enough.

She never let negativity stop her. She showed me that if you hold on to your dreams, you can aspire to things considered outlandish in your small town. She did it at the age of sixty-nine on *The Price Is Right*. That's comforting because I'm now seventy and still waiting for my ham and smart-ass skills to pay off.

Unfortunately, the woman who raised me, loved all her children fiercely, and was our relentless promoter, was also the source of my embarrassment. She was a walking, talking, very loud billboard for Italy in a cotton print dress with a produce-stained apron. And I was trying my hardest to be the normal American child of the 1950s and '60s that advertising and TV shows made me think I should be.

Cinnamon-Sugar-Topped Zucchini Bread

Makes 2 loaves

This moist, delicious bread will definitely make you feel loved.

INGREDIENTS

3 eggs

2 cups sugar

2 teaspoons vanilla

¾ cup canola or any vegetable oil

3 cups flour

1 teaspoon baking powder

1 teaspoon baking soda

½ teaspoon salt

1½ teaspoons cinnamon

3 cups grated zucchini, unpeeled, drained

1 cup drained crushed pineapple (packed in pineapple juice)

2 to 3 tablespoons butter for top of bread when done baking

Cinnamon Sugar

2 tablespoons sugar

1 teaspoon cinnamon

STEPS

1.   Preheat the oven to 350°F.

2. Grease and flour two bread pans sized 5 x 9 or 4.5 x 8.5 inches. If there's any additional mixture left over, prepare a small cake pan or 2 to 4 small ceramic ramekins or cupcake tins. (You can also make muffins with this recipe.)

3. In a large bowl, beat together the eggs, sugar, vanilla, and oil. Set aside.

4. In a separate bowl, combine the flour, baking powder, baking soda, salt, and cinnamon.

5. Give the zucchini a squeeze by rolling it into a paper towel and squeezing to get excess moisture out. (Don't worry if it's still a bit moist, the bread will turn out fine.)

6. Add the shredded zucchini and the pineapple to the egg mixture. Then add the dry ingredients. Be sure to mix thoroughly, scraping from the bottom.

7. Pour the mixture into the prepared pans, filling them about two-thirds full.

8. Bake, and begin checking the smaller containers after 20 minutes. When the tops are lightly browned and a toothpick inserted in the center comes out clean, the bread is done. The larger bread pans will take longer (at least 40 minutes or so).

9. While the bread is baking, combine the sugar with the cinnamon and mix thoroughly. (If you have an empty spice container, fill it with the cinnamon sugar and set it aside.)

10. Once the bread is done, remove from the oven and while it's still hot, rub the top with a tablespoon or two of butter (regular, not unsalted). Once the top is buttered thoroughly, sprinkle it with the cinnamon sugar. (If you don't have a spice container, just lightly sprinkle it with a teaspoon.)

11. Being careful not to get burned, run a knife or plastic blade along the sides of the bread to make sure it releases from the pan.

12. Once the bread is cool enough to handle, place two pieces of plastic wrap or foil on the counter lengthwise and widthwise (creating a cross) large enough to wrap around the

entire loaf. Turn the loaf pan over onto the plastic wrap and the bread should fall out. If bits stick to the bottom of the pan, just scrape them out and piece together. Then flip the bread over, wrap, and let it cool completely. (It stays moist with the wrap on. That's why we wrap it!) It tastes great warm or cool. Enjoy!

Good Nutrition
Keeps Your Children Alive

y mom provided a nonstop parade of delicious meals in large quantities because:

1. Italians are incapable of cooking any other way.

2. She was keeping herself busy while waiting to strike it rich.

3. Cooking was how she showed love, plus feeding us well ensured we were firing on all cylinders so we could make her proud.

4. She was convinced children needed an extra ten to fifteen pounds to ward off sickness and death.

She felt this way because of what happened to her first child.

Mary and my father, Robert, had only been married a couple of years. They were just getting started and living in an apartment building Mary's parents owned. It was a drafty old building with a bad heating system and not a great place to raise a baby. Mary took her first son to get photos taken in an adorable sailor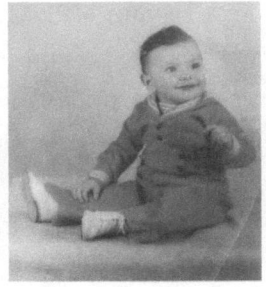

suit in January 1942 and he came down with pneumonia afterward. He was almost ten months old.

My parents tried everything they knew to help. My mom tried breastfeeding him to no avail. They bundled and cuddled him; they even cut onion slices, warmed them, and placed them on his chest—a home-made concoction believed in those days to relieve congestion. All it did was leave red circles on his skin. When Robert and Mary's infant son died at 3:55 a.m., ten months and one day after he was born, Robert, probably delirious from lack of sleep, said he heard angels singing.

A beautiful 8 x 10 of the brother I never knew in that sailor outfit sat in my brothers' room as a perpetual reminder of how adorable he was and what my parents had lost. My mother always blamed herself that he got sick.

Her lack of education left her unable to understand that pneumonia is transmitted by germs in the air and on surfaces. She was adamant that a few pounds and warmth were key to avoiding sickness. The guilt and sadness she felt over his passing never left her, so we knew she was feeding and bundling us out of love.

That's why in winter I was unrecognizable as a human life-form. Snow pants were a must. From November through April, and possibly May (see photo for proof), I didn't go anywhere without flannel pants or leggings under my dress. Leggings of the 1950s and '60s were giant, poufy breeches that made me look like a two-legged dirigible playing in the snow.

The overfeeding extended to our classmates and friends too. After all, their success would influence our success. So when Saint Joseph's Elementary School cafeteria needed volunteers, my mom stepped up to help, knowing she had the right experience for the job. They put her on the serving line and she was thrilled to be there, doing what she did best, feeding children.

Mom was a woman you didn't mess with. She was about five feet tall and weighed about two hundred pounds, a hundred of which she blamed on childbirth. She knew how much weight each of us had put on her and was quick to remind us of that if weight was ever mentioned. Her belly was as perfectly round as a meatball, restrained by the hardest-working girdle in town. Her wavy black hair was held back with glossy black bobby pins. In the '60s she wore the shiny silver, or sometimes gold, cat's-eye glasses that were popular. She had strong heavy arms and hands, and folded you in a hug, even if she was meeting you for the first time. So when she said "Eat!" you ate.

In the cafeteria Mom worriedly scrutinized kids pushing their trays through the line, proclaiming, "Oh, honey, you're skin anna bones, you better eat!" Then, like a one-woman Red Cross, she filled their plates with the amount she thought was necessary to pull them back from the brink of starvation.

Later that afternoon she was politely removed from the serving line.

Growing up in Italy, she learned that you always offer hospitality. In our New Brighton home, hospitality meant you invited visitors in, made them comfortable, and offered food and drink. Mom took it one step further and basically force-fed guests until they begged her to stop. She was determined to show benevolence whether her company wanted it or not.

So whether you were visiting one of her kids, dropping off a package, or just stopping by to get a paper signed, she'd cajole you into sitting down and eating something. "Oh come on, a honey, you gadda eat a someteeng a," she'd say, like it was the law. She frequently told us, "Iffa you love a me, you'll eat."

She'd race to the downstairs kitchen meat slicer and cut a pound of salami before guests could get their napkins open. At a time when TV moms greeted children with warm cookies and a smile, my mom was in a housedress and apron, shoving a plate of salami and cheese in my friends' faces.

If the victims/guests didn't eat enough, she'd give them a dejected look and ask pointedly, "What's a matta? Don'd you like a my food?" My friends learned saying no was not an option. She was both comforting and a little scary.

Ma Tunno's Bread
Makes 8 loaves

Because you have to have something to serve with that salami and cheese! Plus, you can use it to make the other two recipes below, Mom's Festival Roll and delicious fried dough, which Mom called *pizzelle*.

INGREDIENTS

4 cups milk

2 cups water

2 large cakes of yeast, or 3 packs of dry Quick-Rise

½ cup sugar

2 tablespoons salt

½ cup vegetable oil

½ cup melted butter

4 pounds flour (approx.)

STEPS

1. Warm the milk and the water and mix it in a very large bowl with the yeast. The milk and water mixture should be warm but not hot. The milk and water mixture should be warm but not hot. "Just a warm enuffa so you can a smear it uppa wit a you hands" was how Mom described it to me. (About 110–120°F, but no hotter or you'll kill the yeast.) Make sure the yeast dissolves.

2. Add the sugar and salt to the warm liquid mixture and stir until it dissolves. Add the oil and melted butter. Add 8 to 10 cups of flour and mix until the dough becomes sticky. Then pour the dough onto a well-floured surface.

3. Continue adding flour and gently knead the dough until it no longer picks up flour, about 10 minutes. Rub the dough all over with vegetable oil so it doesn't harden. Put it in a large oiled bowl covered with a clean cloth in a warm space, and let it rise.

4. After the dough doubles in size, remove it from the bowl and knead again for a minute or two on a well-floured surface. Then make small loaves and place them in greased pans. Cover the pans with a clean cloth and let the dough rise again before baking. Put the loaves in the oven and bake at 350°F for 45 minutes, or until uniformly browned. If you like a harder crust, lightly spray the top of the dough with water during the first 10 minutes in the oven.

5. Take the bread out of the pans and let it cool. If you like a soft crust, brush the crust with butter.

Festival Roll

Makes about 20 (1-inch) slices

Second in my heart, after Mom's pizza, was her killer invention, the festival roll. Homemade bread dough was rolled out flat and thick, then covered with sweet Italian sausage, pepperoni, chopped hard-boiled eggs, chunks of ham, grated cheese, and lots of mozzarella. She'd roll it up and bake it on a greased cookie sheet until it was golden brown. The cookie sheet was necessary because the roll was so huge it wouldn't fit on anything else. It sat giant and U-shaped with hot cheese bubbling out like Jabba the Hutt of delicious baked goods. Make this with the bread dough and they'll love you forever!

INGREDIENTS

6 to 8 cups Ma Tunno's bread dough (see recipe above)

1 cup pepperoni slices

1 cup cooked loose sweet Italian sausage bits

1 cup ham, cut into small ½-inch chunks

2 hard-boiled eggs, chopped into small pieces

½ cup Parmigiano or Romano cheese

2 cups grated mozzarella

STEPS

1. Roll the dough out on a floured board until it's about 15 inches round but not too thin, three-quarters of an inch thick. Use more dough if it's too thin.

2. Place the pepperoni all over the dough, followed by the sausage and ham. Then sprinkle the chopped eggs over the other ingredients. Sprinkle it lightly with Parmigiano, then liberally with the mozzarella.

3. Start at the bottom of the dough and roll it up into a roll. You may have to moisten the edges to get them to stick together to seal the loaf. Carefully pick it up and place on a greased cookie sheet, folding it into a U to fit the sheet.

4. Cover it with a clean cloth and set in a warm place to rise. Once it's risen, bake it at 350°F for 20 to 30 minutes, or until golden brown.

Fried Dough Sprinkled with Sugar
(Mom's Pizzelle)

Makes 1 large, or two small

This is way better than a platter of TV mom cookies.

INGREDIENTS

2 tablespoons vegetable oil

1 cup Ma Tunno's bread dough (see recipe above)

1 teaspoon (or more) sugar (you can sprinkle with cinnamon too if you like)

STEPS

1. Place 1 tablespoon of the vegetable oil in a frying pan on medium heat.

2. Roll out the dough with a rolling pin until it's about the size of a medium tortilla, about ½ inch thick.

3. Place the rolled dough in the hot oil and cook, turning it until it's light brown on both sides.

4. Remove the fried dough from the pan, sprinkle with sugar, and serve warm.

Sickness Was No Laughing Matter

No matter how well Mom fed and took care of us, sometimes we got sick. That upended her whole Kids Make You Proud plan, which threw my mom into a frenzy of worry and prayer.

My father, also raised in Italy, had no discernable accent, or home "remedies" like my mom. He proudly spoke of his time in the US Army during World War II and sprang into action using his army medic training. In the fall he applied a disgusting, medicinal purple paint to the backs of our throats, to ward off sickness, or used sulfa powder left over from the war if we got a scrape. If I woke up vomiting, he was the one who got out of bed and came to the bathroom, gently holding my forehead as I wretched.

My mom had her own reliable cures. She might:

1. Empty us of food.
2. Fill us up with food.
3. Knock us out with spiked tea.
4. Smother us in Vicks VapoRub.

5. Combine prayer with medieval spells (learned during her formative years in Naples).

In fifth grade, Bernie told Mom he was sick because he hadn't studied for a test and thought he could get out of it. Her immediate and all-time favorite diagnosis was constipation, which did not rule out going to school. None of us could miss school unless we were actually dead.

Mom felt emptying Bernie of food was the cure, so she gave him some Ex-Lax, saying, "Dis issa chocolate, you eat it, you feel a better in no time." But Bernie knew what Ex-Lax was and was afraid he might not make it to the bathroom on time.

He said, "Ma, I just can't run to the bathroom when I want!" She responded, "Don't a worry, Bernard, I write a note and a you can go wenna you have to go . . . OK, honey?" Bernie figured this wasn't bad. He could "have to" go in the middle of the test and look up the answers in his hidden notes. Bernie, who was enrolled at the same Catholic school my mom attended for a short time, clearly wasn't taking his Catholicism seriously.

As soon as he got to class, he gave the note to Sister DeLourdes and went to his seat, waiting to see if it worked. She smiled, chuckled, snorted, turned red, and dashed out the door. Bernie says she told the class to study for the test.

He looked past the door and saw her laughing with some other nuns, so he ran up, wondering what was in the note Mom had written. Here's what he remembers:

Dere Sistre,

Pleaz xcuz my lilla Bernard today if he gotta go to da batroom real quik to take a shit! I gave hem a fizik and he cod have to shit at any time. He's a gooda boy.

Sencerly,
Mrs Mary Tunno

Bernie was dying of embarrassment but heard the rattle of rosary beads signaling a nun was coming, so he ran back to his seat. Sister came back for the note and Bernie says he heard more cackling in the hallway from the other nuns.

We can probably assume Sister DeLourdes saved Mom's masterpiece for nun-show-and-tell back at the convent. After that, he never let her write another note. They made a deal: He would write the notes, and she would sign them. Her writing did improve slightly by the time I was in school, but Bernie taught me two valuable lessons: never fake sickness, and write your own notes.

Since filling someone with food was much more in line with her *Eat a lilla some a ting, it'll make a you feel a better* philosophy, she'd begin cooking at the first sign of illness. If it was an upset stomach, she made white rice with milk and a dash of cinnamon, or she whipped up vanilla pudding. If it was a sore throat or a cold, chicken soup was started immediately.

"Honey, I'mma gonna make you some a chicken soup—you feel better in a no time," she'd say. Thirty minutes later, the delicate aroma of chicken and vegetables would envelop every corner of the house, and in little more than an hour the soup would be ready to eat.

I'd drag myself to the dining room table and let the steam from the hot soup caress my face before I tasted my first perfectly salted spoonful. Even now, when I taste it, it's like she's hovering beside me holding a bottle of booze, a jar of Vicks, and her favorite red rosary beads.

Hot tea spiked with lemon, honey, and Rock and Rye was part three of filling us up with something to cure us. Rock and Rye is rye whiskey sweetened with rock candy. This was the early '60s, before parents learned the ugly truth about alcohol killing brain cells.

Jacquin's Rock and Rye (our family favorite) has sliced fruit and cherries in the bottle as a consolation prize when you finish the whiskey. It's sweet enough to rot your teeth, but you're so relaxed you don't care.

June Cleaver would have been horrified, but hot Lipton tea with lemon, honey, and Rock and Rye helped me see a clear advantage to being my mother's child.

Vicks VapoRub was another sickness-fighting favorite. Mom insisted on applying a thick coating of it to my chest and back when I had a cold, so I had to lie still, like a buttered dinner roll, knowing any sudden move could slide me out of bed and right onto the floor. When sickness is on the line, a woman's gotta do what she's gotta do.

Sometimes that also involved medieval spells. America in the 1950s and '60s wasn't famous for medieval treatments, but there was still a fair amount of superstition mixed with Catholicism in Sparanise, Italy, when Mom was a girl. So she learned an incantation or two, along with reading, writing, cooking, crocheting, and embroidering. My father referred to it as hocus-pocus.

I got a lot of headaches as a child. My mom was convinced this was because of "bad eyes," or *malocchio*. Neapolitan wisdom claims that *malocchio* strikes when someone is thinking of you, possibly with envy (giving you the evil eye), and the only way to get rid of it is the time-tested water and holy oil method. If she was out of holy oil, Mom substituted Wesson or Crisco. I thought everyone's mom did this.

As soon as I mentioned the headache, she'd start praying, give me some aspirin, and make me lie down on the couch. (This was before doctors learned that aspirin can cause Reye's syndrome. Honestly, it's a miracle that with aspirin, no seat belts, no car seats, no airbags, no bike helmets, spiked tea, and kids riding in the backs of pickup trucks for fun that any of us made it to adulthood.)

Once I was on the couch, Mom got a soup dish, filled it with water and got out her little bottle of holy oil. She'd say several Hail Marys over the dish, then put her thumb in the holy oil and let the oil drip from her thumb into the water. As she did this, she prayed, saying *"Squagliare malocchio"* (liquefy bad eyes) three times while making the sign of the cross. That was the cure. If it was a really bad headache, she'd put holy oil on my forehead in the shape of a cross for extra potency.

When I woke up, the headache was usually gone and I'd feel a grease slick on my forehead. She always took credit for the cure, saying, "Oh, Frenzy, you hadda *malocchio* real bad, but I took a dem off, come and see."

She said that if the oil drops spread out when they hit the water that meant you had a pretty serious case. Afterward, I'd walk to the kitchen and look in the soup dish, but it never looked like anything more than a soup dish with water and oil in it. I clearly never had her gift. However, I did manage to live to see all the ways she pursued fortune and fame, both legally and . . . not so legally, so maybe there was something to her methods.

Mary Tunno's Healing Chicken Soup
Serves 8 to 10

If this doesn't cure you, you better head to the Emergency Room.

INGREDIENTS

1 carcass of a rotisserie or baked chicken with substantial meat left on

3 to 4 quarts water

1 cup coarsely chopped celery including inner leaves

½ cup chopped fresh parsley

1 medium to large onion, roughly chopped

2 to 3 medium carrots, coarsely chopped, or 1 cup baby carrots

½ cup tomato sauce, or 1 fresh tomato, peeled, seeded, and

pureed (optional)

Salt and pepper

½ to 1 cup egg noodles or pastina (optional)

STEPS

1. In a large pot over high heat, add the chicken and water with the celery, parsley, onion, and carrots, and let it boil. Skim off any foamy residue. Lower the heat to medium and let the soup simmer about an hour, or until the meat is falling from the bone.

2. Remove the skin and meat from the bone. Discard the skin and bone, chop the meat into one-inch pieces, and return it to the soup.

3. Add the tomato, if using, and salt and pepper. Bring the soup to a boil again and add the egg noodles. Stir the soup occasionally so the noodles don't stick, and serve it when the noodles are tender.

4. Sprinkle the soup with grated cheese for extra goodness.

5. You can also substitute premade, vacuum-packed, or frozen gnocchi or dumplings for the noodles. A dumpling recipe follows.

Dumplings

Makes about 4 medium

INGREDIENTS

1 cup flour

1 teaspoon salt

1 teaspoon baking powder

¼ teaspoon dried thyme (optional)

2 tablespoons butter, melted

½ cup milk

STEPS

1. In a medium bowl, mix the flour, salt, baking powder, and thyme.

2. Add the butter and mix; then add the milk a little at a time, until the dumplings hold together. They should be sticky but not runny.

3. Drop them in the gently boiling soup (see recipe above) using a tablespoon or ice-cream scoop. (They grow as they cook.)

4. Cover the pan, turn the heat to medium/low so the soup gently boils, and let them cook for 15 minutes. Serve hot.

Mom's Comforting Vanilla Pudding

Makes 3 to 4 (½ cup) servings

Mom's cure for the upset tummy. It's easy and delicious!

INGREDIENTS

1½ cups 2% or whole milk

2 tablespoons whipping cream

2 egg yolks

2 tablespoons cornstarch

¼ cup sugar

1½ teaspoons vanilla

STEPS

1. In a small saucepan over medium heat, combine all the ingredients and stir with a wire whisk.

2. Continue stirring until the mixture begins to thicken.

3. Once it's thickened, serve it warm, or cover the pan and let it cool in the refrigerator.

A Born Contestant

Years before my mom dreamed of coming on down, she pursued different ways to win prizes and money. Some were legal, others . . . not so much . . . like playing the numbers. Did that stop her from participating? No, nothing can stop a woman who's convinced she's destined to be a winner.

Before the legal lottery system was established in Pennsylvania in 1972, the not-so-legal system called the numbers racket flourished in working-class neighborhoods. Often it was carried out in barbershops, shoe repairs, mom-and-pop stores, or by an entrepreneurial neighbor. Someone collected the money and placed the bets. The winning number, or daily number, was the last three digits of the total volume of the daily New York Stock Exchange trades.

In the mornings, Mom wrote her bets down on a small piece of paper, put her nickels and dimes inside, rolled the paper up, and gave it to Bernie. On his way to Catholic school, Bernie stopped at a local shop, handed the paper with money inside to the local bookie (I mean entrepreneur), and the bets were placed. Every so often Mom won, but mostly she didn't. Sometimes she'd dream of a number, play it, and win.

Considering the odds were 999 to one, I'm impressed she ever won. I'm even more impressed she never got arrested.

By the time I was in grade school she had a mathematical system she called the workout, where she thought she could figure out the daily number. This was impressive optimism for a woman who didn't finish elementary school. She commandeered the black-and-white composition folders I brought from school for her workout calculations. I'd find them with every square inch filled with numbers. She also relied on dream books, which interpreted the meaning of dreams and gave you a handy three-digit number you could put your money on.

Much to my brother Bob's dismay, she'd made a connection with a bookie/entrepreneur, who was the mother of one of Bob's college friends. My mom called her regularly to play whatever numbers she wanted.

If she didn't win, she'd gripe, "Dammit, I hadda dat number right here!" Then she'd point to one of a million numbers in my stolen notebook to show me proof. Of course, the number was there: *every* number was there.

Mom's habit caused some friction between my hardworking, honest-to-the-core dad and freewheeling mother. She always said, "I don't drink, I don't smoke, I don't drive, I don't go to da beauty shop—dis issa de only ting I do." But she knew she was jeopardizing her marriage, and it had to stop, or at least slow down. Luckily, there were also legal paths to prizes.

In 1964, the *Beaver County Times* sent keys attached to each daily newspaper for something called the Treasure Chest drawing. It featured a chained-off area in the Sears store at our local shopping center, Northern Lights. The area had a padlock, and if your key opened the padlock, you could choose any of the items inside. There was a mattress set, a window air-conditioner, a sewing machine, and a few other items Sears probably needed to clear out.

My mom persuaded her sister, my aunt Blanche, to drive to Northern Lights so they could try their keys. My mom and aunt walked into

Sears and went straight to the padlocked area. Mom looked heavenward, said a quick prayer, and tried her key.

When the lock opened in her hand, the entire store heard a very loud "OOOOOHHHH, JESUS!" Store personnel came running and Mom reveled in her moment of victory, memorialized with a photo in the *Beaver County Times*.

TREASURE CHEST WINNERS — Mrs. Mary Tunno, New Brighton, stands beside the sewing machine she won during the Treasure Chest promotion at Northern Lights Shopping Center. With her is George Ranies, Aliquippa, advertising manager at Sears Roebuck & Co. ... Mrs. Tunno's key opened the lock permitting her to choose one of the gifts on display. Keys were located on the front of a special tabloid section of the TIMES on March 9. Keys may be tried in the locks in the various stores in the shopping center through today. Most stores are open until 9:30 p.m.

Mom could have picked any of the wonderful prizes inside the chained-off area. It was March, so she must have forgotten that our house heated like a sauna in summers. There was a perfectly wonderful air-conditioner sitting right in front of her, but what did she choose? The Sears Kenmore cabinet sewing machine in a lovely walnut finish. Did she have any idea how to sew on one? No.

It came with a series of free lessons, which she guilted me into attending. "Honey, you gadda come," she said. "I'mma gonna feel too nervous wit a dose American ladies trying to eck a splain tings to me."

One night a week for a few months my dad dropped us off at Sears, where we sat in a small white room with about eight sewing machines manned by genteel women and learned the basics. We learned the parts of the machine, how to thread it, how to sew a straight line and a zigzag stitch, and did our best to master some simple skills in spite of Mom's puzzlement over the term *zipper foot*. "Honey, why dey call dis a foot?" she asked loudly. I shushed her and explained that it did kind of look like a foot, but she never got it. At the end of our classes, and after considerable effort, she turned out a nice-looking white apron with pink scalloped stitching.

Emboldened by her success in the apron category, she thought she could just take apart one of her dresses, follow the pattern, and make a new dress. She worked with a white fabric with bright yellow polka dots for weeks, then decided to give us a fashion show.

She emerged from her bedroom in what might mercifully be called a shift. It was two pieces of material with holes cut for sleeves and perky pieces of fraying fabric tying the material above each shoulder. This yellow-polka-dotted splendor of a dress hung on her like a sack and she knew it. This presentation was definitely for entertainment purposes only.

The sun filtered through the sheer living room curtains as she smiled and twirled her way into the room, doing her best imitation of a runway model. Seeing the look of wonder/shock on the faces of me, my dad, and my sister, she doubled over in uncontrollable laughter, ending the show and her sewing career.

It also ended the working portion of the sewing machine's life. After that, it sat in the dining room not realizing its fate would be intertwined with the holy Catholic Apostolic Church and show business.

Pasta e Ceci (Mom called it Ceci di Pasta), a.k.a. Pasta e Fagioli

Makes about 4 servings

This was my mom's go-to comfort food, perfect for disappointment over any unsuccessful attempt at fashion design.

INGREDIENTS

1 medium brown or white onion, or 5 green onions

5 large cloves garlic, minced

2 tablespoons olive oil

1 (15 ounces) can chickpeas (Do not drain!)

½ pound pasta (elbow pasta is good or *tubetti* (tiny tubes)

1 tablespoon fresh basil, chopped

½ (28 ounces) can Cento Italian whole peeled tomatoes (Be sure to take the seeds out of the tomatoes, then puree them before adding them to the mixture.)

Salt and pepper

STEPS

1. Place a pot of water on the stove to boil. While waiting, slice the onions and chop the garlic.

2. In a large skillet over medium heat, add the olive oil and sauté the onions and garlic, 2 to 3 minutes.

3. Add the chickpeas (with liquid) and sauté until they are heated through.

4. Add the processed tomatoes and let the mixture heat through.

5. Add the pasta to the pot of boiling water.

6. When it's done, drain the pasta thoroughly and add to the skillet; mix the pasta with the sauce thoroughly. Add the salt and pepper to taste. Once combined and seasoned, serve the pasta with grated cheese.

Jesus, MFT
(Marriage and Family Therapist)

Mom and Dad weren't about to let the children they worked so hard to raise right burn in the fires of hell, so Catholicism and all its trappings were mandatory. Plus, if any of us messed up, there was always a higher power to turn to. And we all know children behave better when they're being stared at by a ceramic concave Jesus face with eyes that suspiciously follow you no matter where you try to hide.

What's even better is a light-up Jesus in a faux gold frame that you won at an amusement park because you are a winner . . . but I'm getting ahead of myself. First, let me explain that my mother was not just religious, she was the Catholic church's dream.

It was impossible to walk into any room of our house without bumping into a baby Jesus, a Blessed Virgin, or a Saint Somebody. Rick, a friend from college, who was also an Italian Catholic, was visiting once and sat stunned at the dining room table. He looked around, amazed at the number of religious icons just in our dining room and kitchen. I challenged him to an icon-off—a timed race to see who could find the most icons. He was good, but I had home-field advantage, so it wasn't really fair. We counted forty religious articles in our kitchen and dining room alone.

I spotted them quickly because I was in charge of cleaning them and had bought many from Sister Claver's religious-article store at school. Business was brisk, especially leading up to Christmas and Mother's Day.

My favorite was my mother's tiny, two-sided plastic TV of the saints with slides inside. On one side is the impeccably dressed Infant of Prague. When you flip it over, you see Saint Anthony. Next flip, Saint Theresa replaces the Infant of Prague until about fifteen different saints show up on TV.

Mom originally wanted to become a nun, but went on a retreat once and made a grim discovery. "All a dey ate was a dat a damma oat-a-meal, morning, noon, anna night." She concluded, "Dis issa shit for da birds."

The Catholic church dodged a bullet with that decision, and my mother passed up her chance to be a nun for a life with better food, but she never lost her love of Catholicism. You might think that forty-plus icons would have been enough, but you would be wrong. Mom's Catholic fervor grew to a frenzy when she was able to combine her two favorite things: winning and Jesus.

My mother attended our elementary school picnic at Idora Park and used her winning ways at a game booth. She walked away proudly carrying home a framed, "light-up" picture of Jesus.

You don't normally see "light-up" Jesus pictures at amusement parks, but they must have gotten wind that the Catholic school kids and their parents were coming, so they stocked up. While my cousin Nancy and I were riding the WildCat roller coaster over and over again, my mom and aunt Blanche were cleaning up with games of chance. Aunt Blanche took home a light-up Jesus too.

In the picture, Jesus looks very celestial: one hand is over his flaming heart, wrapped in a crown of thorns, and one hand is pointed toward heaven. A gilt frame surrounds him, and there's a small light at the top where his eyes look heavenward.

As soon as Mom got home, she put Jesus on her recently won cabinet sewing machine. Then she purchased a giant, glow-in-the-dark rosary with beads the size of grapes.

You might be asking yourself, *Why would anyone need a giant glow-in-the-dark rosary with beads the size of grapes?* (Yet another amazing Catholic marketing moment.) It must have been for those pitch-black nights when Mom wasn't sure whether she was on a Hail Mary or a Glory Be. But since I never saw her pray with it, I think she just draped it around the frame for dramatic effect.

As soon as Jesus arrived, Mom created a new rule. The last one to bed at night had to say, "Good night, Jesus," and turn off the light over Jesus's eyes. If you were the first person up in the morning, it was your job to turn on the light and say, "Good morning, Jesus." She eventually gave up the ritual because she said her "stinking" kids kept forgetting. She just kept Jesus's light on day and night, replacing bulbs as they burned out.

Jesus served as Mom's savior, companion, and therapist. Sometimes, I'd see her on her knees, right there in front of the sewing machine in the dining room, praying a novena. A novena is a special prayer you say for nine consecutive days, for something you really need help with.

Often, she'd be in the middle of mopping the dining room floor when I'd see her pause in front of the sewing machine and say, "Jesus, ha come a my stinkin' husband don't wanna take a me anywhere? Talk a some a sense into him, OK?" Or "Jesus, please make my kids do dare best inna school so dey canna be successful." Also heard was "Jesus, please letta me win onna da number today." Of course, a frequent request was "Jesus, please letta me get onna *The Price Is Right* and be vittorious!"

Light-up Jesus was quickly surrounded by a procession of porcelain and plastic saints, a stack of novena prayers, vases of flowers, and photos of family, all in a specific order, and all on top of the sewing machine. Sewing became impossible. By the time I cleared Jesus, the rosary beads, the prayers, Saint Anthony, the Blessed Mother, Saint Jude, Saint Theresa, and fifteen others away, along with the doily and the prayer books, I didn't care that what I had was ripped; somehow, I'd manage. And if I didn't put everyone back exactly the way she had them, I'd hear an admonishing "Jesus don'd a like it a when a you do datta!"

Jesus and his entourage made their big move when the cabinet TV died. My parents never got rid of furniture; they just moved it and repurposed it. So the cabinet TV got moved into the dining room, giving the saints room to spread out. And the sewing machine became the TV stand, holding the TV that broadcast *The Price Is Right*.

Jesus and friends remained a fixture in the dining room, blessing every juicy, after-mass Sunday ham and every plate of delicious pasta for decades.

Years later, when we were clearing out my parents' home, none of my siblings stepped up to claim Jesus so He was almost tossed into the dumpster. I was stunned and shrieked, "Are you kidding? You can't toss Him out! How can you get rid of Him?" Even my formerly aggressive, now-churchgoing sister didn't step up to claim Him, so I became the lucky owner of light-up Jesus.

Finding the right spot for Him was a decorating challenge, but how could I throw away such a family treasure? His encyclopedic knowledge of my mom's most ardent prayers and Italian curse words makes Him a definite keeper . . . if I could just get Him to talk. But He is a good listener and great in a pinch when my therapist isn't available.

Mom's Sunday Ham with Pineapple, Cloves, Apricot Preserves, and Rock and Rye
Serves 12 to 15

This ham is the perfect combination of sweet and salty and gives you something to be thankful for in church.

INGREDIENTS

    1 large bone-in half ham (7 to 10 pounds)

    15 to 25 whole cloves

    1 can of pineapple rings (save the juice!)

    7 to 10 maraschino cherries

    1½ cups light brown sugar

1 cup apricot or peach preserves

2 to 4 tablespoons pineapple juice

1 tablespoon maraschino cherry juice

¼ cup Rock and Rye whiskey

STEPS

1. Preheat the oven to 350°F. Place the ham in a foil-lined pan with enough foil to fold over, so it's completely covered.

2. Pierce small holes in rows (three to four rows) along the top of the ham and stick the cloves in.

3. Place the pineapple rings on top, securing with toothpicks. Place one cherry in the middle of each pineapple ring. Take the brown sugar and press it into place over the pineapple rings and cloves, evenly coating all of them.

4. Mix the preserves with the pineapple juice, maraschino cherry juice, and Rock and Rye until the preserves are liquid enough to pour.

5. Pour the preserve mixture over the ham. Cover with the foil and let the ham bake for 3 to 4 hours.

An Italian Parents' Guide to Obedience via Terror, Intimidation, Guilt, and Corporal Punishment

My parents knew they couldn't count on our success unless we learned obedience. They'd been through the 1918 pandemic, the Great Depression, and World Wars I and II, so terror, intimidation, guilt, and corporal punishment were no big deal. My mom was a master of all four and gifted in the art of muscling her children home.

Kathy Pfleghar, who lived across the street, was my childhood best friend. If she was playing at my house and her mom wanted her to come home, Mrs. Pfleghar called out with a slow, drawn-out "Kaaaaathy!" If it was urgent, Mrs. Pfleghar calmly telephoned and asked my mother in a nice, civilized TV-mom manner to send Kathy home.

My mother preferred a crescendo approach—her own twist on Ravel's *Boléro*. If I was playing at Kathy's, she'd start out sweetly with a "Fraaanzy" or two. She'd wait a minute, then call out, "Sweetheart, dumpling, lovable, sweet, sweet, sweet!" If I didn't respond, then louder—two octaves higher and with less patience—came *"Fraaaaanzes!"* If there was still no response, she'd add a nice dollop of bitterness and even more volume to the next **"FRAAAAAN . . . ZES!"**

By the next call, she would have lost any semblance of sweetness and screamed, ***"ZÒCCOLA . . . PUTTÀNA, VIENI QUA!"*** In my mother's dialect, that meant "Sewer rat, whore, come here!" Fortunately, our Anglo-Saxon neighbors didn't understand Italian.

Mom's Vesuvius-like ability to go from sweet to serial killer in seconds was a skill finely honed through years of child-rearing. It explains why one minute she could be hugging me and calling me "Da best a lilla gal inna da whole a world," then suddenly smack me on the head and yell, "I'm a gonna choke a you, you lilla *stronzolla*" (which I think translates to "you small female turd").

See how culturally beneficial this book is? You even get Italian lessons. *Strónzo* is the word for *turd* in Italian, but *stronzolla* is decidedly more feminine, although not necessarily a real Italian word. Mom said swearing never sounded as bad in Italian as it did in English.

When I finally heard her cursing me, from my reclined position on Kathy Pfleghar's lawn, I'd pop up like a prairie dog and bolt across the green grass toward home, yelling in explanation, "My mother's gonna kill me!"

If you came through the side door, which I stupidly always did, you entered on a landing. From there, you could either go downstairs to the basement or up three steps to the kitchen, where my help was always needed. Sure enough, she'd be waiting behind the side door, large spoon, or spatula in hand, ready to smack me as I flew through.

Her favorite weapon was a large metal spoon with a melted burgundy plastic handle, giving it a gnarled, ominous look. It was used for draining liquid from pasta and had small, round holes in the spoon part that left a perfectly symmetrical polka-dot pattern when it impacted skin.

"Aaaaaaay, ha come a you don't come a when I call a you? What's a matta . . . you deef?" she'd yell as she perched on the top step, hovering over the doorway. She swung wildly as I scrambled up the three steps to the kitchen, dodging thwacks from the spoon as I went. (This could explain why so many Italians become accomplished boxers.) The good news is she rarely landed a blow; I was much too fast. She was mostly bluster, and I knew it.

Once I helped her, she'd feel guilty for losing her temper, apologize, then go back to thinking I was destined for greatness. A delicious dinner usually followed, like chicken with oregano, crunchy potatoes, carrots, and onions. The gnarled spoon came in handy for scraping up potatoes too.

As it cooks in the oven, the onions caramelize and the potatoes toast up brown and crunchy in the juices from the chicken and the olive oil. The skin of the chicken turns a golden brown. She'd use her spoon/weapon to scrape the potatoes from the bottom of the pan, and I went after every crispy one. I knew I was going to need sustenance if I was going to make it through childhood and survive my mother's Italian freestyle homemaking.

Chicken with Oregano, Potatoes, Onions, and Carrots
Serves 6

This delicious dinner (along with bobbing and weaving skills) was the reward for coming home and facing the spoon of death.

INGREDIENTS

1 package of chicken fryer parts, or 1 whole chicken cut up, or 8 chicken thighs

5 medium red or 2 large Idaho potatoes, cut into small wedges

2 medium onions, cut into slices ½ inch wide

15 (or more) baby carrots

⅓ cup olive oil

2 tablespoons dried oregano

Salt and pepper

STEPS

1. Preheat the oven to 350°F. Rinse and pat the chicken dry and place in a large bowl.

2. Slice the potato wedges into ½-inch slices and place in the bowl.

3. Add the onions and carrots to the potatoes.

4. Drizzle the olive oil over the ingredients and sprinkle liberally with the oregano and salt and pepper to taste. Toss to combine so every piece is well seasoned.

5. Place the ingredients in a greased 15 x 11-inch pan or cookie sheet with the skin side of the chicken down.

6. Cover the pan with aluminum foil and cook in the oven for 1.5 hours.

7. Discard the foil, turn the chicken, and let the skin brown in the oven for 30 to 40 minutes, or until nicely browned.

8. If you want the potatoes crunchy, remove the chicken and carrots from the oven, keeping them warm, then drain the excess liquid and leave the potatoes in, uncovered, for another half hour until they crisp up.

Italian Freestyle Homemaking

Game shows give people something to hope for. While my mom was slaving away, she could at least dream of winning a new car, dining room set, washing machine, or hundreds of yards of new carpeting. Even watching other people win was a daily shot in the arm of hope while she was stuck doing mundane chores like cooking, cleaning, laundry, and ironing. But there was no law that said she had to enjoy them or be good at them.

As a child, I never gave a thought as to whether Mom was a happy homemaker. Kids are generally selfish that way. I just wanted some semblance of that tidy, organized American home I saw on TV.

Unlike everyone else in my family, I was fixated on organization before I could even read. At four, I was organizing the papers in my father's desk drawers according to color. I wanted our house to run with Swiss precision, like the Pfleghars across the street. They had washing days, ironing days, daily menus, a whole set of encyclopedias (not just the A's that were free at the grocery store with your purchase), plus bath times and bedtimes!

At nine years old I actually begged my parents to force me to go to

bed at 9:00 p.m. like my classmates. I remember them distractedly looking up from the TV and saying, "Uh, OK, go to bed," without a hint of a
threat, then going back to watching TV and ignoring me. When you're
the fifth kid, apparently parents just think, *OK, we've got this,* and mostly
quit worrying.

Our house was run in what I call the Italian freestyle method, meaning there was no method. Mom was always ready to cook or bake, which
was great, but we had to wait until she *felt* like doing less fun chores like
laundry or ironing. When would she do them? We never knew. So it took
a while from the time your clothes went into the laundry basket until
you saw them again—if you saw them again. Quite often they came back
unrecognizable.

The days I came home from school and smelled Clorox bleach, I
knew she'd been doing one of her least favorite things—laundry. If my
mother had any sadistic tendencies, besides spatula-wielding, she hid
them well until laundry day.

I'd smell the bleach, glimpse through the breezeway window, and see
crisp white sheets, work shirts, and my mom's girdles flapping in the backyard breeze. Then panic struck because I knew I was probably too late.

My mother was a serial clothing abuser, and Clorox was her weapon of choice. She washed our clothes in a white 1950s Maytag wringer washer in a sinister-looking corner of the basement where the furnace sat. The corner, lit by an uncovered light bulb with a pull string, sat waiting for my mother or a wandering KGB agent who needed a place to torture someone.

The first load was the whites. Dressed innocently in a housedress and apron, Mom placed a hose from the basement sink into the washer and filled it with scalding hot water.

The white Maytag was shaped like a square wine barrel with legs. In front was a knob you pulled out when you wanted the agitator to rotate back and forth to wash the clothes. You pushed it in to stop it.

Not only was the water scalding hot, but Mom poured the Clorox liberally. She cut brown Fels Naptha soap into little pieces and added it to the water with her favorite detergent, Tide. Fels Naptha was a 1960s version of a pre-soaker and stain remover. It's also described as a skin irritant, something that in retrospect, explains a lot.

Next, she had to pull the clothes out of the scalding hot water with a long, round wooden dowel and send them through the wringer, being very careful her fingers didn't go with them. Sometimes, she'd send too many in and the top of the wringer would pop up, just like the head of a Rock 'Em Sock 'Em Robot when you landed a good punch.

The clothes then went into the deep sink filled with rinse water, then through the wringer again, then were stuffed into the laundry basket and taken outside to be hung on the clothesline.

A skilled laundress would empty the washer of the hot Clorox water by placing the machine's drain hose into the drain on the floor and letting the water pour out. Then refill the washing machine again with nice cool water for the brightly colored clothes.

My mother was not a skilled laundress, nor did she feel it was right to waste perfectly good water. So she reused the hot Clorox water for the next load (the unfortunate, multicolored clothes). I can still see them in their pile on the cold, concrete floor, desperately screaming, "No, take the darks!"

The formerly bright, cheerful colors all took on a pathetic pallor once Mom got through with them. I remember the tragic sight of a favorite sweater, once a lovely light blue in the right size, reduced to toddler size in a sickening yellow.

I longed for Kathy Pfleghar's clothes. I remember glancing in her closet once and sighing at the sight of four or five shirts, hanging in perfectly pressed perfection.

As soon as I learned to wash clothes, I'd race downstairs at the first scent of Clorox to save whatever hadn't been plunged into liquid hell. My mom may have not finished elementary school, but she knew how to get us to do our own laundry very early. I started at six.

My first-grade photo is proof of my skills. I'm in the front row to the right of blue-eyed Bobbie Jo in the center. She's in black tights and a striped sweater looking adorable, the epitome of 1960s hip cuteness.

I'm in a dress with black ribbons across the bottom, and one of my mom's holy medal pins front and center. I ironed that dress (yes, I learned to iron at an early age too) so I'd be ready for my close-up. I spread my dress out, so everyone could see my fabulous ironing job. But the lady taking the photo told me to tuck it under so I didn't cover the other girls' outfits, although I did hog a little space from Bobbie Jo and Debbie Hogan to the left of me. At six I was already on my way to diva-hood.

Starching followed the washing. When I got home from school, it was my job to stand on a chair at the downstairs gas stove and stir a giant pot of boiling water mixed with Argo Corn Starch and a waxy blue rectangle of Satina (an ironing aid) until the Satina melted. (There are so many possibilities for irreparable burning and scarring in that paragraph alone, it's truly a miracle I survived childhood.) Then the starch was ready.

Once the clothes were washed, my mom used the wooden dowel

to dip shirts and dresses into the hot starch, then put them through the ringer. Once dry, our clothes could stand at attention.

Ironing day was much less traumatic. After school, as soon as I opened the side door, I could feel the steam and knew what Mom was up to. Our starched clothes had to be dampened so they could be ironed. Advanced ironers used soda bottles with holes poked into the cap as a sprinkling device. My mom used her hand and a pan of water. She'd cup her hand in the water, then liberally sprinkle each piece of clothing in front of her. Each besprinkled dress or shirt was rolled into a tight cocoon and added to a mountain of clothes on the clear plastic sheet that covered the dining room table.

If I saw one of my dresses at the bottom of the pile, I'd pull it out and put it on top, so there was a chance it would make it to my closet that day. It was a thrill to see a dress in my closet clean, pressed, and ready to go.

Mom would sit transfixed by *General Hospital*, yelling at sad-eyed Jessie Brewer not to trust her stinking husband, Dr. Phil Brewer. "Don'd a geeve in to him; he's a no good louse!" but Jessie never listened. Mom's heavy arm moved the iron slowly back and forth as the wooden ironing board creaked. Sometimes she'd pause at a dramatic moment and I'd watch, holding my breath, worried she might scorch something.

In hindsight, I have to give her credit. If I had to go through all that for my kids' clothes, they would have never seen them again, so even once a month was pretty good. One of her happiest moments had to have been the day we retired the wringer washer and got her a modern washer and dryer. The upside is she gave us laundry skills.

Although Italian freestyle homemaking cuts down on your clothing choices, it opens up wonderful food possibilities. The time Mom didn't spend on laundry was usually spent making something fantastic, especially during the holidays.

Her delicious homemade cannoli were my favorite pastry. She made them for special occasions like Christmas, Easter, nun bribery, or whenever she felt like it. When I eat them, I can picture her standing right beside me, saying, "Have anoder one, honey, dare good!" I'd rather have them than a pile of ironed shirts any day.

Mama Tunno's Cannoli

Makes approximately 15 to 25 cannoli

These cannoli are crunchy, light tubes of pastry with just the tiniest hint of wine, filled with creamy, sweet ricotta flavored with a dash of cinnamon and studded with chocolate chips. Sprinkled with powdered sugar, they're absolutely delicious.

(Don't fill the shells until you're ready to serve them, or they'll get soggy. And read the directions below before starting because the ricotta should be drained before mixing it, or it might be too runny.)

INGREDIENTS

2½ cups flour

1 tablespoon sugar

¾ to 1 teaspoon salt

½ cup plus 1 tablespoon Butter Flavor Crisco (plain Crisco works too)

2 eggs, plus 1 beaten in a separate cup for making the cannoli stick together

3 ounces white wine (chardonnay is fine)

40 ounces canola oil

STEPS

1. In a medium bowl, mix the flour, sugar, and salt.

2. Once the dry ingredients are combined, add the Crisco, mixing it with your fingers or a pastry cutter.

3. Once it's pebbly, like pie dough, add 2 eggs and the wine. Mix well with your hands until combined. Wrap the dough in plastic so it doesn't dry out.

4. In a large skillet or deep fryer, add the canola oil. Heat it to 375°F. Lightly grease the outside of six metal cannoli tubes.

5. While the oil is heating, roll out the dough to pie-crust thickness, or slightly thinner, about one-eighth of an inch. With a rolling cookie cutter, cut a circle in the dough about 6 inches in diameter. Wrap it around the cannoli tube, and where it overlaps, rub some of the beaten egg to seal the cannoli shell together. They don't need to overlap much.

6. Carefully place the covered tube into the hot grease. Let it fry for 3 to 5 minutes, or until it's golden brown. Carefully remove it from the pan. You can cook a few at once, but I didn't fry more than three so I could keep an eye on them. Once the tubes have cooled enough to touch, gently remove the metal cylinders, grease their outsides, and repeat the process.

Cannoli Filling

My mom put citron in hers, but I'm not a fan, so I don't. Feel free to chop up a teaspoon of it and add it to each of the flavors of filling, if you want more authentic cannoli.

Vanilla Filling

INGREDIENTS

1 (32 ounces) container of Galbani ricotta (This is the absolute best for cannoli; it's smooth and not gritty!)

¾ to 1 cup powdered sugar

2 to 3 sprinkles of cinnamon

⅔ cup mini chocolate chips

1 to 2 teaspoons finely chopped citron (optional)

STEPS

1. Place the ricotta in cheesecloth and allow to drain in the refrigerator for 2 to 6 hours; otherwise, it can be a little runny.

2. With an electric mixer, whip together the ricotta, powdered sugar, and cinnamon until creamy.

3. Add the mini chocolate chips, mixing them in by hand until they're incorporated.

4. Separate the filling into two parts. Use half to make the chocolate filling (recipe below).

Chocolate Filling

INGREDIENTS

½ cup chocolate chips, melted

2 tablespoons whipping cream

½ the vanilla filling (see above recipe)

1 to 2 teaspoons finely chopped citron (optional)

STEPS

1. Melt the chocolate chips in the microwave or on the stovetop, and add the whipping cream.

2. Mix until smooth, then blend into the separated half of the vanilla filling.

Now comes the fun part. Find two clean plastic Ziplock bags, or two pastry bags. Fill one with chocolate filling and one with vanilla. Snip off one end of the plastic bag and squirt the vanilla ricotta filling into one end of the cannoli and the chocolate into the other side. Sprinkle with powdered sugar and serve. Do not fill until ready to serve because they get soggy. If you like, you can dip the ends into chocolate chips or pistachios, but I like them plain. Enjoy!

Can Food Be Embarrassing?

Yes.

The 1960s were famous for:

a. Miniskirts

b. Rock and roll

c. Political upheaval

d. Hunting and gathering

e. All of the above

If you didn't answer (e) "all of the above," you clearly did not live with my family in the swinging '60s. Fresh produce from our garden was one means of keeping us fed, but certainly not the only one. Foraging was my mom's signature spring and summer ritual. What our neighbors were poisoning, Mom was turning into salad. If you haven't figured it out by now, food eclipsed everything in our Italian family and kept my mom busy year-round.

I remember looking out the window of the bus as it slowly pulled up to our house and cringing. It was springtime, and there was my mom, bending over picking dandelions in the front yard and stashing them in her apron. A peek at the right moment exposed the garters from her girdle struggling to hang on to her nylons. This was back in the early '60s, when women wore things like nylon stockings, girdles, and garters, not because they were trying to be sexy but because comfort hadn't been invented yet.

I nervously eyed the kids on our school bus, praying no one noticed her. It was bad enough she was unfeminine, but seeing her out there harvesting was like putting a sign in our front yard exclaiming, "Hey, we're so poor we have to eat weeds!" Why couldn't we just poison our dandelions like everyone else? I thought, *God, if we just had more money, we could go to the grocery store and buy iceberg lettuce like our neighbors. Why do we have to supplement with stuff from the yard? Why can't we have weekly menus with normal food like tuna casserole, hamburgers, and ham loaf like the blessedly American Pfleghar family across the street?* Mom didn't care what I thought or what the neighbors thought. Every spring she picked the dandelions, called *cicoria* in Italian, and made them into a salad.

The hunting was even worse. More than once, I wandered into the garage, daydreaming like a kid should, and came face-to-face with a dead, gutted deer, strung up by its back hooves, with its tongue hanging out, like a frat boy after a rough party. My dad and brothers stood there posing for pictures with the poor thing, as if they were prom dates.

We also had lots of rabbits in backyard pens. My sister and I played with them daily. I thought they were pets, until they became dinner guests, and not in a jacket-and-tie way. If you're squeamish, or a card-carrying member of PETA, you should probably skip the next three paragraphs.

On execution day, Dad and Mom took the rabbits into the basement. Dad held the rabbit upside down by its hind legs and hit it hard behind the ears with his hand once or twice. When it was dead, they slit open its belly as entrails spilled onto newspaper that was spread on the basement kitchen floor. Watching from the top of the stairs, I'll never forget the sickening splat of rabbit entrails hitting the paper.

My parents viewed the rabbits as food, so killing them was just something that had to be done. Since then, I've learned my dad's method is one of the most humane ways to kill a rabbit. But it was still pretty awful to watch, and seeing it once was enough. I could never have done it. My mom tried to hide the truth and always told me it was chicken, but I knew it was rabbit and wouldn't touch it even though she disguised it with wine and onions.

It was the same fate for the occasional goat that arrived in the spring. Thankfully, I must have blocked out witnessing those executions. And if a couple of chickens suddenly showed up in the basement with my mother, I knew it wasn't going to end well. My parents were nice people who committed a fair amount of murder.

When they weren't on a killing spree, they gardened. Dad worked stinky manure into the soil every spring, then planted. Their seed-planting reflected their personalities. My father planted in neat rows, while my mother just threw seeds wherever she damn well pleased.

Dad came home after laying brick and block all day, tilled and weeded the garden, and tied up tomato plants with scraps of old rags as sweat dripped from his face. If you ever suffer from low energy, it's because my dad got every ounce the universe had to offer.

Spring through summer, I'd wake to find my mother sitting at the dining room table, reading the paper and having a cup of coffee. Her white nurse shoes, loved for their comfort, sat looking defeated by the kitchen door. They slouched wet from the morning dew and were covered in grass. She'd already been through the garden to pick what was ripe.

In spring, the sink was full of bright green onions, crisp asparagus, fresh lettuce, and other produce. By May we were eating my mother's decadent omelets filled with asparagus, green onions, chunks of ham, and creamy, melted mozzarella or *scamorza* cheese. In summer there were beans, broccoli, zucchini, and zucchini blossoms, cauliflower, plus mulberries and nectarines. In fall came dozens of tomatoes, apples, pears, and plums.

My parents spent late summer through fall canning tomatoes, peaches, pears, nectarines, and plums, and turning apples into pies and apple sauce. On damp September days Dad would go into the woods and come home with sheepshead mushrooms that grow on decaying oak trees. They also turned the sweet Concord grapes that dangled from the grape arbor over our basement door into juice and wine.

The basement door opened to a backyard that sloped gently down to the woods. Carefully laid stones lined the walls on either side of the door. Overhead hanging clusters of grapes and dark green leaves created a beautiful canopy. One of the delights of August and September was standing under the grape arbor during a light rain and picking a bunch of ripe purple grapes. I loved squeezing each grape out of its skin and feeling it pop slippery into my mouth, sweet as candy, while I listened to the rain and stared into the lush green woods.

Like many Italian families, we had two kitchens. One upstairs for everyday use, and one in the basement when it was too hot for summer cooking and canning upstairs. God forbid, we should miss a home-cooked meal because of summer heat.

In July and August, when the heat and humidity were sweltering and normal kids played in swimming pools and sprinklers, my parents made me and my siblings pick blackberries in the woods with them. We dressed in suffocating long-sleeved shirts and pants to avoid being scratched. Insects hissed as blackberries plinked against our metal pans. We were a small-scale Libby's with forced child labor. Once home, Mom made juicy blackberry pies and sweet, dark ruby jam. Peaches, pears, nectarines, plums, green beans, zucchini, and beets also got canned for storing in the wine cellar.

I didn't want to eat dandelions, or the mushrooms my dad picked, but once I tasted them, they were really good. I hated picking blackberries, and in truth probably ate way more than I picked, but my mom's pies and jam were absolutely delicious.

Mostly, all this work kept our household of six fed, which was a miracle because we ate a lot. We anticipated the bounty of the coming months and felt connected with each season and cycle. Anything that can connect you with seasons and cycles and doesn't involve the word *menstruation* is a good thing.

Scrambled Eggs with Asparagus, Green Onions, Ham, and Cheese
Makes 4 servings

Spring is a beautiful time of year anyway, but eating these eggs with melty cheese, onions, ham, and asparagus makes you even more thankful for it!

INGREDIENTS

6 large eggs

1 tablespoon half-and-half or milk

1 to 2 tablespoons olive oil

6 asparagus stalks, rinsed (ends broken off) and chopped into 1-inch pieces

6 green onions, chopped into 1-inch pieces

8 ounces ham, cubed

3 to 6 ounces fresh mozzarella or soft white cheese, like *scamorza*, cut into 1-inch pieces, ½ inch thick

Salt and pepper

STEPS

1. Place the eggs in a small bowl, add the half-and-half, and mix well. Set aside.

2. In a skillet over medium, heat 1 tablespoon of the olive oil about a minute.

3. Add the asparagus and green onions to the skillet.

4. Cook until almost tender, then add the ham until heated through; then add the eggs and cheese.

5. Scramble together and continue cooking over medium heat until the cheese is melted and eggs are cooked.

6. Serve immediately. Add salt and pepper to taste.

Sautéed Sheepshead,
a.k.a. Hen of the Woods Mushrooms

Makes 4 servings

You can find hen of the woods in September or October after a good rain. They grow on decaying oak trees. But don't expect your Italian friends to tell you where they are, because they are very secretive about the location of a good stash. (If you've been overzealous and picked too many, you can squeeze the water out and freeze them for cooking later.)

INGREDIENTS

1 pound sheepshead mushrooms, cleaned and broken into small pieces

2 tablespoons olive oil

1 tablespoon butter

3 cloves garlic, minced

Salt and pepper

STEPS

1. After rinsing the mushrooms thoroughly (they can hold a lot of dirt), drain them well.

2. Place the mushrooms in a large pot of water and boil for 20 to 30 minutes to be sure all the dirt is out.

3. Remove from the water, let them cool, and squeeze the excess liquid out.

4. In a skillet over medium heat, add the oil and butter, then the garlic and squeezed mushrooms.

5. Sauté 10 to 15 minutes; then add salt and pepper to taste and serve.

The Night I Finally Grew Up . . . a Little

When I was fifteen, the combination of my mom's accent, education, hairstyle, personality, and weight made me cringe when my friends were around. Common wisdom holds that anything that embarrassed you as a kid will make you ten times more embarrassed as a teenager. So Mother-Daughter Night, sponsored by the Girls Athletic Association, was not an event I wanted my mom to attend.

I said, "Oh, there'll be girls with their mothers in the gym. They'll be playing volleyball and basketball in shorts and running around playing other games. I don't know what you'd do there, but if you want to come, you can."

I heard the disappointment in her voice as she said, "You don't a want a me dare. I'll a look a like a big a buffalo with all a dose skinny mothers." Then with sad resignation, she looked at me and said, "It's OK, honey, you go without me. Have a good a time."

A good daughter would have felt terrible, but I was relieved. I knew she wouldn't be able to play like the other moms. And I didn't want the embarrassment of everyone knowing my mom was more like everyone's grandmother. Plus, she was always telling people how wonderful I was and I was afraid we'd both be laughed at.

So she stayed home and I went to the GAA night with my best friend Carolyn, her young, thin mother, and a little something my mom sent along. All night, I watched mothers in blue jeans and shorts doing acrobatic leaps as they played volleyball. Everyone looked like they were having a great time.

While I played, my self-absorbed teenage brain kept thinking, *Why can't my mother be like this? She's never been cool like these mothers. Why did she have to wait until she was forty-two to have me?* (Like it still would have been me if she'd been twenty.) *Why does she have to be overweight? Why does she still have that dumb accent?* I felt alone and very low all night. Then it was time to eat.

Since my mother knew she wasn't joining, she did what she usually did, she sent a little something. Her idea of "a little something" was two pizzas the size of large cookie sheets. She had baked the pizzas the day before, and they became her ambassadors.

After everyone finished playing, we settled down in the gym bleachers for snacks. I brought out the pizzas my mother had carefully wrapped in aluminum foil. I checked them for weird ingredients because occasionally I'd come home, smell something delicious and garlicky, open the oven door, and recoil at the sight of a split goat head sizzling away inside. Since Mom never wasted anything, I had to make sure a goaty surprise hadn't slipped onto a pizza.

They checked out, so I sliced them, passed them around, and waited, hoping people liked them. Everyone ate and things were quiet for a while.

Then I heard whispers. Mothers, daughters, even Miss Dietrich the gym teacher started asking about the pizza. Where did it come from, who made it, and where could they get more? Everyone was raving over it and telling me how lucky I was.

They said none of them ever got homemade pizza, let alone pizza this good. I couldn't believe it. In minutes my mother became the most praised and possibly the most famous mother in the history of GAA Mother-Daughter Night without touching a volleyball. Oohs and aahs echoed throughout the gym. The way these people carried on you'd have thought they'd never had pizza before.

I went from feeling like a pathetic orphan to the luckiest teenager in New Brighton. And the pizza wasn't even hot. It was cold, day-old pizza!

Later that night I sat alone in the dark bleachers, staring at the brightly lit gym floor and felt ashamed. I felt guilty for all the times I'd wished my mom had been someone else, someone cooler, thinner, normal and American—someone who didn't roast goat heads.

Then I made a vow. *I'll never resent my mother for who she is and what she doesn't do anymore. She does something just as important as the "normal" moms, she's just in a different talent category.*

When I got home and told her how much everyone loved her pizza and how lucky they said I was, she beamed. I thanked her and it was the beginning of a new chapter between us.

Mom's Thick-Crust Pizza

Makes 8 large pieces of pizza

Make this and your kids will definitely start appreciating you.

INGREDIENTS

4-5 cups of Ma Tunno's bread dough (see recipe on page 46)

1 (28 ounces) can Cento Italian whole peeled tomatoes

1 to 2 teaspoons dried oregano

1 cup sliced pepperoni

Parmigiano or Romano, grated

Mozzarella, shredded

STEPS

1. Preheat the oven to 350°F.

2. After the dough has risen once, take a portion (4 to 5 cups) and roll it out flat on a floured surface, so you get a thick crust.

3. Place the dough onto a large cookie sheet. (Mom put hers on a greased cookie sheet.) It's very difficult to get it to stick to the sides when the sheet is greased, but with patience you can do it.

4. Since Mom's homemade tomato sauce isn't commercially available, use Cento peeled tomatoes with basil (*pomodori pelati*); it is the closest I've ever come to hers. The basil gives the tomatoes a nice flavor. Seed the tomatoes, then puree.

5. Pour enough tomato sauce on the dough to cover it.

6. Sprinkle on a little oregano—not too much, just lightly to season.

7. Then add the sliced pepperoni.

8. Sprinkle some Parmigiano cheese on top.

9. Cook the pizza on the bottom rack of the oven for 15 to 20 minutes.

10. Add the mozzarella cheese on top of the pizza in the final 5 to 10 minutes of baking.

11. Check the bottom of the pizza to make sure it's lightly browned.

When a Dream Takes Hold

Dreams can take hold at any time. Sometimes it'll even surprise you. There you'll be in the middle of entertaining your guests when one of them blurts out that your dream doesn't have an ice cube's chance in hell of coming true. That's when, come floods, pandemics, or pestilence, you know it has to.

That's what happened to my mom. I knew she loved winning and being the center of attention, but she always seemed to be happy with what she had. She always said, "I couldn't wanna anyting a more. I got a beautiful house, a good a husband, anna good children. I couldn't a be happier." So I didn't think her talk about *The Price Is Right* was anything more than a fan enjoying the show.

But she did have a dream she shared one Ladies' Night.

Ladies' Night happened once or twice a year. It was the night she and her group of mostly Italian card-playing friends got together and played 500. The group included Mom, her sister Johanna, mom's cousin Annie, and several friends. Sometimes Aunt Johanna's daughter or Mrs. Pfleghar would fill in for a missing lady. The night was a big deal, so Mom and I started cleaning the house two weeks in advance. My father started sharpening his color commentary about that time too.

We took apart couches, vacuumed, mothballed, and left them without slipcovers for that one magic night. Furniture was polished and topped with clean, starched white doilies.

My mom scrubbed our rose-colored living room rug on her hands and knees. We washed and waxed the hardwood floors. We took apart beds, vacuumed, and put on dust ruffles and my mother's delicate, hand-crocheted white bedspreads, which no one ever got near because they were packed back into storage as soon as the ladies left.

Ladies' Night was the only night Mom ever used her vast China teacup collection. Delicate bone china cups, some with tiny pink painted roses, some with large yellow roses, and some with gold-painted handles and rims that stood tiptoe on three tiny, gold-painted feet. The table was covered with one of Mom's finest hand-crocheted tablecloths, and we always got a brand-new piece of clear plastic to cover the table because nothing was too good for the ladies.

In the early years, Mom would bake a ham, serve broccoli with lemon and butter, make scalloped potatoes, then serve pineapple upside-down cake or pie for dessert. But the ladies decided the heavy meals were too much for their waistlines, so Mom was reduced to making warm chipped ham and Velveeta sandwiches for their after-game snack.

When the ladies arrived, I had to look presentable, answer questions politely, and take each of their sweetly perfumed coats and hang them in the closet. Under no circumstances was I to sneak any Brach's candy or salted mixed nuts from the glass candy dishes on the card tables.

Then I was banished to the basement with my dad and had to stay there until I was called to help or the ladies had gone. Every time the ladies squealed with laughter, my dad said, "What the hell do those battle-axes have to talk about for three hours when they get together?" He'd mimic them, then mumble, "They sound like a bunch of damned chickens."

It irked him that he was banished to the basement of the house he'd built because of the ladies. But, in spite of his Archie Bunker reactions, he went along with it because, deep down, he knew he got to go hunting with the guys, or do whatever he wanted, and Mom deserved to have fun too because she worked as hard as he did, just in a different way.

I think having daughters started to open his eyes to how unfair life could be for women. He told me that when he was growing up in Italy, women were treated like a man's property, even his own mom. Men made the decisions and women had to go along with them. He knew that just wasn't right. He and my mom discussed everything and made all their decisions together.

The night Mom's big dream took hold was a Ladies' Night in the early '70s. It left her fuming. The ladies were listening to my mother raving about *The Price Is Right*. She was telling the ladies how much she loved the show and wanted to be on it and meet her idol, Bob Barker, sounding hopeful she would.

One of the ladies thought my mother sounded ridiculous and said, "What makes you think *you* have a chance?"

Her comment left Mom furious. After the ladies left, she spat out, "How dare she say datta to me!" Those old feelings of not being good enough rolled over her again, leaving her feeling gutted and more determined than ever. All she kept saying was, "Oooohh, I'd a like a to get onna dat a show anna plug her mouth! Jesus, please give a me da chance!"

Think what you will, but I think her light-up picture hotline to Jesus helped that plea cut through the clutter.

Chipped Ham and Velveeta Sandwiches
Serves 18

This will give you something to stuff in the mouth of anyone who dares to say your dream has no chance! Yes, there's Velveeta in these sandwiches and, yes, I loved them as a kid. Hey, it was big in the 1960s and '70s! But I suppose you could substitute shredded cheddar, if you must. Chipped ham is a popular item in Pittsburgh. It's very thinly sliced boiled or pressed ham . . . and it's delicious!

Chipped Ham Filling

INGREDIENTS

> 1 ½ pounds chipped ham, coarsely chopped
>
> 4 hard-boiled eggs, diced
>
> ½ cup mayonnaise
>
> ½ cup ketchup or chili sauce
>
> 2 tablespoons mustard
>
> 1 cup Velveeta cheese, diced
>
> 18 hamburger buns

STEPS

1. Preheat the oven to 350°F.
2. Mix all the ingredients, except the buns, thoroughly.
3. Divide the filling among the buns and wrap in foil.
4. Place the wrapped buns on a cookie sheet in the oven and bake for 15 to 20 minutes, or until the cheese is melted.

My Catholic guilt won't let me leave this chapter with one recipe you may only be able to make in Pittsburgh. So I'm adding one of my very favorite recipes. It doesn't fit with the theme, but I don't care because it's really good. You're gonna love this!

Bob's Fettucine with Scallops in Curry Cream Sauce
Serves 6

This is my Christmas Eve favorite, created by my brother Bob, and it's great for any family who likes to celebrate *la Vigilia*, or the Feast of the Seven Fishes.

INGREDIENTS

    5 cloves of garlic, minced

    ½ cup butter

    ½ cup olive oil

    2 tablespoons finely chopped parsley

    1 bay leaf

    1 teaspoon finely chopped fresh (or dry) rosemary

    ½ teaspoon dried basil, or 1 teaspoon finely chopped fresh basil

    ¼ teaspoon dried oregano

    1 pound of bay scallops

    4 fluid ounces dry sherry

    1 pound fettucine pasta

    1 teaspoon curry powder

1 pint heavy whipping cream

Salt and pepper

STEPS

1. In a large skillet over low heat, sauté the garlic in the butter and oil, and add the herbs.

2. Add the scallops to the butter-herb mixture and sauté until opaque. Remove the scallops from the heat and set them aside.

3. Add the sherry to the butter-herb mixture, and let it cook down about 5 minutes.

4. In a pot of boiling water, cook the pasta.

5. In the skillet, add the curry powder and whipping cream. Cook an additional 5 minutes, returning the scallops to the pan for the last minute to heat them through.

6. Drain the pasta thoroughly, add it to the skillet, and toss to make sure it's thoroughly combined.

7. Pour the pasta into a serving bowl.

8. Add salt and pepper to taste.

9. Serve the pasta with grated Pecorino or Parmigiano Reggiano and crushed red pepper.

Teaching Optimism

When I buy lottery tickets, or enter contests, I fully expect to be a winner because my mom taught me to be an optimist. She knew optimism is what keeps a person going when things go south. One of her favorite sayings was "Columbus took a chance."

My optimism has led to a fair amount of disappointment, but it hasn't stopped me, even though I'm not the leader of the free world or the starlet she imagined I would be (and at seventy, it's not looking terribly promising). But I keep plugging away at smaller dreams. Something more in line with my ham and smart-ass skill set.

Mom knew optimists are the only ones who have a chance in life because pessimists are already defeated by their attitude. In spite of the snarky comment from her card-club lady, she never gave up hope on *The Price Is Right* or any contest.

Receipt for Articles of Eligibility

Be it confirmed that
MRS. UBALDO TUNNO
is the rightful recipient of attached Sweepstakes Articles which define eligibility and prizes in the Reader's Digest $275,000.00 Sweepstakes.

00712 69781   22871

One of her favorite legal contests was Publishers Clearing House. *Reader's Digest* was another gem along with tons of other mail-order houses that held contests and sold incredibly cheap things like plastic coasters with birds on them and cheerful yellow corncob salt and pepper shakers made of plastic.

She ordered these flimsy trinkets (sorry, Mom, I mean very special prizes) thinking the order gave her a better chance at winning whatever the *very, very* special prize was. She was lured in by important letters from catalog companies, seldom noticing they almost never spelled her name correctly. They went something like this:

> *Dear Mrs. Mary Tommo,*
>
> *You are our special winner!*
>
> *Just order three items from our catalog and you'll automatically be entered in our Million Dollar Contest! Yes, Mary Tommo, you could be the lucky winner of One Million Dollars!*

That simple message was all it took. "Butta, Frenzy, honey, why would a these a people write a me dissa letter and tell a me dis if a dey don't a think I have a chance a to win?" she naively asked. I

tried to tell her about sales, profits, trickery, and greed, but she was certain she was destined to be a millionaire and would hear none of it.

She saw things in catalogs and ordered them, rarely checking their dimensions, then she'd get angry that they'd sent her what she ordered because it looked different in the picture. She'd say, "Dissa stuff looked a so nice inna da book and when I get it, it's nading but a cheap a plastic."

To not become a millionaire on top of being bamboozled into buying junk was just too much for her, so she needed to lash out.

Since I was the youngest and still tethered to home until sweet college freed me, I was the reluctant scribe who had to write a reasonable-sounding letter while she dictated an angry tirade. "Da hell with it! Frenzy!" she'd shout. "Send it a back wit a note a dat a says, I don't a want a dissa shit!"

Knowing a little something about a proper business letter, I thought her approach lacked subtlety. I tried reasoning with her, explaining that usually she got exactly what she ordered, which really ticked her off. Finally, she'd admit she didn't give a damn about being reasonable. She just wanted her money back.

She'd say, "OK, Frenzy, you write a for me dissa letter." Then she'd stand at the dining room table angrily gesturing and hollering her letter at me, while I did my best to transcribe fury into reason at lightning speed.

You dorty rotten skongs, *(Dear Sirs:)*

I'm a pooty damn angry about a dissa lousy cheap a junk a you have sent a me yesterday.

(I received your merchandise yesterday and, unfortunately, it's not what I had in mind.)

I'm a sendin' all dissa junk a back. You gypped a me and I wanna alla my money back right a now.

(Enclosed, please find the merchandise I'm returning and please credit my account for the returned items.)

Go take a shit, *(Sincerely,)*

Mrs. Mary Tunno

This translation had to be done quickly because once she was on a roll she was unstoppable. She'd be done yelling and I'd still be on "you gypped a me." Irritated, she'd say, "Frenzy, can'd a you write aney faster?"

Clearly, this was not a job for a thin-skinned person, or a stranger. Which is why my sister and I were stunned when Mom approached Patty, the girl my brother Bob had been dating, whom he finally got up the nerve to bring home for Thanksgiving. Bringing anyone home was always fraught with danger for any of us, but it was a special kind of danger for my brothers, for the following reasons:

1. Whoever she was, she would never be good enough for my mother's Italian sons/kings. (More on that later.)
2. She had to be Italian, Catholic, or both.
3. She could possibly be a *puttàna*—any girl who dated my brothers was suspect, in which case my mother's usual hospitality disappeared. (Bernie brought a girl home once who dared to sit too close to him on the couch and Mom turned to ice.)
4. If Mom did like her, the badgering over when a marriage would take place would never end.

Patty, or datta gal, as in, "Tell a datta gal to eat a some more turkey," was sweet and fun. My mother liked her immediately and picked her up off the ground in a big hug as soon as she walked up the three steps into the kitchen. Mom enthused, "She's a so cute and she has such cute lilla legs!"

But later, after dinner, when we saw Mom pull out her receipts and say, "Patty, honey, do you tink you can a help a me wit some a ting?" my sister and I cringed. We looked at each other and slinked away like the miscreants in *The Godfather* who took off right before the car exploded and poor Apollonia was toast.

Around the corner, we waited in fear, listening. Patty sat patiently with my mom, who explained, as meekly as a lamb, at normal volume (because she wanted my brother to marry datta gal): "Dis damn a cheap a stuff is not a what I ordered. Honey, can you write for me dis a letter?" Patty remembers writing a couple of letters and changing them to a kinder, censored version. My sister and I were amazed that she got off totally easy with no wild gestures or yelling, and minimal cursing.

The concessions a mother will make to ensure her son marries a nice girl . . . and he did.

Fran's Scrumptious, Juicy, Dry-Brined Turkey
Serves 8 to 10

I send my thanks to Russ Parsons, former *LA Times* food writer, for starting me on the dry-brined turkey trail. I will never go back.

INGREDIENTS

1 (15 pounds) turkey

3 tablespoons kosher salt

2 tablespoons fresh rosemary, finely chopped

1 tablespoon lemon rind

STEPS

1. Thaw the turkey in the refrigerator first. It takes a day to thaw 5 pounds of turkey, so 3 days should take it from bowling ball hard to soft and pliable. Once thawed, rinse it thoroughly, removing giblets. Then pat it dry inside and out.

2. Mix the kosher salt, rosemary, and lemon zest thoroughly. Then sprinkle the inside of the turkey lightly with the seasoned salt. Place the turkey on its back and salt the breasts, concentrating salt where meat is thickest.

3. Turn the turkey on one side and sprinkle the entire side with seasoned salt, concentrating on the thigh. Flip the turkey over and do the same on the other side.

4. Place the turkey in a Reynolds turkey-size oven bag. Squeeze out the air and seal tightly. Place the turkey breast side up on a pan (in case it leaks) in the refrigerator for 3 days. Leave it in the bag, but turn it daily and massage the seasoned salt into the skin. The turkey will see more action than you will . . . I'm just sayin'.

5. On the day it's to be cooked, remove from the bag and let it sit out at room temperature for an hour. Follow the directions below for the stuffing.

Rosemary, Lemon, Garlic Roast Turkey with Sausage-Chestnut Stuffing

Serves 6 to 9

INGREDIENTS

1 (15 pounds) turkey, already dry-brined

15 large roasted chestnuts, chopped into ½-inch pieces, or chestnuts in a jar (from Williams-Sonoma)

1 pound sweet Italian sausage, loose, not in casings

2 boxes Stove Top Turkey Stuffing mix (I know it's prepackaged, but it's really good!)

3 cups water

½ cup butter

2 to 3 stalks celery, cut into ½-inch slices (2 cups)

1½ cups (3 sticks, unsalted) butter for rubbing

4 tablespoons finely chopped fresh rosemary

1 tablespoon finely chopped garlic

1 tablespoon lemon zest

STEPS

1. Preheat the oven to 350°F. Remove the turkey from the refrigerator and take it out of the plastic bag. Massage it thoroughly, dry it, and set aside at room temperature for an hour.

2. You can use the canned chestnuts, or fresh ones you'll have to roast. If using fresh, cut an X into each chestnut and roast them in the oven for about 45 minutes, or until tender. Skin them and chop into ½-inch pieces. Set them aside.

3. In a skillet over medium heat, brown the Italian sausage until it is no longer pink. Drain on a paper towel and set it aside.

4. Prepare the Stove Top stuffing mix as directed.

5. In a large pot over medium heat, warm the water and butter until butter melts.

6. Add the celery, chestnuts, and Italian sausage to the stuffing mix and combine thoroughly. Add additional water up to ⅓ cup, if it's too dry. Cover the stuffing with a lid and set aside.

7. Soften the butter and add the rosemary, garlic, and lemon zest. Mix thoroughly. Set it aside.

8. Make sure turkey has been dried inside and out with a paper towel. Place the turkey, breast side up, in a large roasting pan greased with olive oil or cooking spray. With your hand, gently work your way under the skin of the turkey breast so there's a pocket. Then insert 2 tablespoons of the butter-rosemary-garlic-lemon-zest mixture into the pocket on each side of the breast. Press down on the skin so it's evenly distributed.

9. Take the rest of the butter mixture and rub it all over the outside of the turkey, breast, back, thighs, and wings.

10. Stuff the stuffing mixture into the cavity of the turkey as well as the area near the neck. Do not pack it too tightly. If you have some left over, grease a small casserole dish, place the stuffing into the dish, cover and refrigerate it, then cover with foil and heat in the oven, 40 minutes before dinner is ready.

11. Find a large piece of clean, 100% cotton material and wash it thoroughly so it does not smell of fabric softener. (A large, old white T-shirt with no writing on it is perfect.) Rinse it thoroughly, then wring, leaving it very damp but not dripping. Lay the cotton material over the turkey so it covers it completely, and place it in the oven.

12. Check on the turkey every half hour, removing the cloth, basting the turkey, then placing the cloth back over the turkey and thoroughly spraying the cloth with water until the cloth is wet. Do this until the turkey is golden brown on top and juices run clear. About 4 hours.

13. Let the turkey rest for at least 20 minutes before carving it.

Mom's Turkey Stuffing with Ground Beef, Mushrooms, and Cheese

Serves 6 to 8

After transcribing an angry tirade, you deserve this stuffing. And yes, every home should have at least two stuffings!

INGREDIENTS

1 cup onion, diced

1 pound ground beef

5 slices of French or Italian bread, cut into cubes

1¼ cups milk

2 cups chopped mushrooms

1 tablespoon olive oil

2 eggs

½ cup chopped parsley

½ cup Parmigiano cheese

Salt and pepper

STEPS

1. In a large skillet over medium heat, sauté the onion with the ground meat. Cook the onion and ground beef until the beef is no longer pink. Drain the grease, discard it, and set the beef-onion mixture aside.

2. In a medium saucepan over medium heat, add the bread and milk, and stir until the bread is saturated and almost creamy. Set it aside.

3. In a separate pan, sauté the mushrooms in olive oil until the water they release is evaporated; then add them to the beef-onion mixture.

4. Add the bread and milk mixture, then the eggs, parsley, and cheese.

5. Add salt and pepper to taste and mix well.

6. Stuff the turkey with this or put it in a bowl, sprinkle it with more Parmigiano cheese and heat it, covered with foil for 20 to 30 minutes. My mother will love you!

Mix Trootfully

One of the ways my mom kept herself very busy while waiting for luck to strike was with baking. And baking is never more important than at an Italian wedding. Thank God, my older brothers took the pressure off when it came to getting married and having children because marriage and grandchildren were both in the top five on Mom's priority list.

In case I haven't mentioned it before, this was my mother's priority list:

1. Cooking / feeding da people.
2. Finding suitable mates for her children.
3. Making sure her children bore grandchildren (preferably boys first).
4. Making sure her daughters remained virgins until marriage.
5. Being a contestant on *The Price Is Right* or striking it rich, a.k.a. winning a million dollars.

When Bernie announced he was marrying Donna, it was right up there with a royal coronation. That's because he was the oldest living boy in our Italian family, which is akin to being king. If there are several boys, they get to be King #1, King #2, et cetera.

This king nonsense stems from the fact that my mother was raised in Sparanise, Italy, from 1913 until 1925, where men had all the power and women had very little.

Boy kings are free from the constraints Italian girls have imposed on them because . . . wait for it . . . they're *boys*! Boys get to go off to college without a fight. Boys never get lectured on virginity and always get to play bocce in the backyard while the girls watch. Boys can camp out in the backyard, take off on road trips without a police escort, always get lavish praise for cooking, rarely have to clean, and get to fall asleep after dinner on holidays without helping with the dishes.

It was why my mom said things like, "Let a da men eat first," which drove me completely insane. She was raised to believe women should serve men and men can do whatever they want, but women can't.

My brothers had chores like cutting the grass, painting the fence, fixing the car, and helping my dad. But the perks of being a male always looked really good to me, and yes, it irritated the shit out of me, even though I love my brothers. (Sorry, that was quite a digression. I clearly need more time with the therapist.)

My mom felt duty-bound to strut her baking stuff at Bernie's reception because even great wedding receptions can get the Italian lady thumbs-down for lack of cookies or a bad selection.

The unwritten rule for Italian weddings is: There should be a minimum of ten to twenty cookie varieties to choose from and a minimum of six dozen of each variety. If the table doesn't loudly groan under the weight of the cookies, your mother credentials are suspect.

As you may recall, my oldest brother passed away in infancy. Then Bernie came along and kept Mom company while the world was at war and Dad was away fighting. He was part of her healing process, and . . . because he lived . . . he was proof she was a good mother. She always said, "When a I see Bernie, I see heaven a." So clearly heaven's wedding was going to require the mother lode of cookies.

Baking those cookies took an entire month and a half in the spring of 1969. My mom was not to be outdone by my aunt Johanna, who'd gone into full-blown baker mode before her daughter's wedding. I remember longingly eyeing the thousands of cookies being stored on tray after tray in a cool area of my aunt's basement, waiting for the wedding day, and plotting which ones I'd eat first at the reception.

Mom and I started baking on May 1, so we'd have enough cookies for my brother's June 21 wedding. We stood in our basement kitchen, staring at the stack of cookbooks Mom kept but rarely used, hoping for inspiration.

We decided on almond tea cookies from the *Cookie Cookbook* because Mom thought they sounded good. We altered the original recipe, eliminating the chopped almonds, using almond-flavored icing instead of tea, and putting a cherry on top instead of an almond. I'm sure the original author of the recipe, Eva A. Beasley, from Portland, Indiana, is beyond caring.

I was about thirteen and had been helping my mom bake since I was five, so we confidently divided the duties. I got out the ingredients, mixed them together, and Mom sat reading the instructions.

We were doing OK. The first four ingredients were in and mixed when I said, "OK, Ma, what's next?" Without skipping a beat, she said, "Adda sifted a flour anna chopped almonds. Mix trootfully."

I looked up, a little puzzled, and said, "What?"

Again, a little impatient and more forcefully she repeated, "Adda sifted a flour anna chopped almonds. Mix trootfully!"

Trootfully . . . trootfully. I'm thinking, *What can she possibly be reading?*

I asked one more time, "Ma, are you sure it's truthfully?"

Maybe the volume of baking ahead got to her because she went serial killer on me and yelled, **"Gaddamit, a Frenzy, I don'd a know, but it says a right a here, mix a trootfully!"** She punctuated her point by pounding her heavy fist on the cookbook, sending up an angry dust cloud of flour.

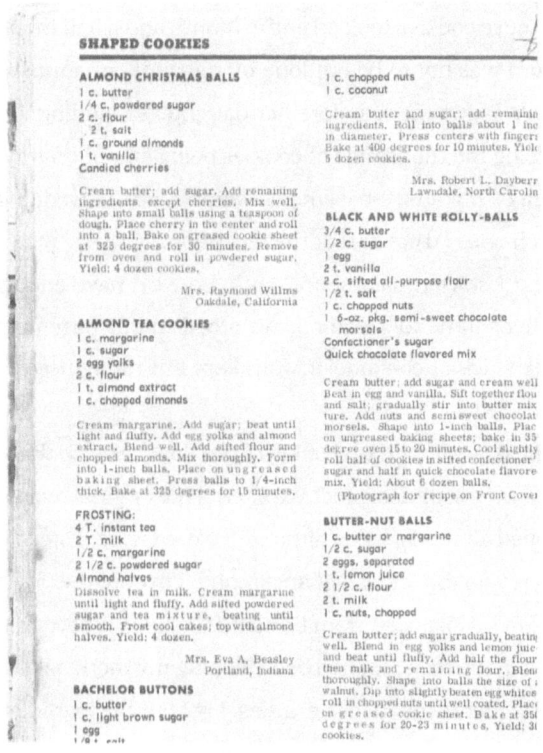

So I put the bowl down, calmly walked over, and looked at the recipe. Ready to be vindicated, she looked up at me expectantly, through the flour-smeared glasses sliding down her nose. Her face was flushed, and she was not happy that I had the audacity to doubt her.

A situation like this held potential danger. She could either start yelling in Italian and smack me on the head (never hard, just enough to remind me who's in charge) or burst into laughter. You never knew. Growing up with her was like training to become an explosive ordnance specialist. I looked at the book and finally understood what she was trying to say.

Trying to suppress my smile, I gently said, "Ma, that's not *truthfully*, that's *thoroughly*. Mix *thoroughly*." Then I waited a beat and asked, "How would you mix truthfully?"

Finally, her brow unfurrowed, her eyes opened wide, and I heard, "OOOHHHHH!" She finally got it. We could never buy my mother funny Hallmark cards because of the language barrier, so anytime she got it with no explanation was a huge victory.

She buried her face in her hands and started a silent shaking laugh. Next, she leaned back, scarlet-faced, and laughed out loud. In seconds, the whole table, nestled against her ample stomach, started shaking furiously back and forth like it was possessed and she was helpless to stop it.

I heard her gasp, "Oh, Frenzy, you keella me," and then she went into another spasm of laughter as the table kept convulsing. The rest of the cookie baking went without incident and I lived to tell the story.

The only dark side to the tale is that after we slaved away, baking for a month and a half, half the cookies were stolen the night of the wedding.

I'm not sure how it happened. Our cookies were delivered early in the day to the kitchen of the hotel venue. The wedding was at 6:30 p.m., so we didn't get to the reception until late. Some cookies were on tables when we got there, but later when Donna asked that they put the rest of the cookies out, they said they'd run out. The bride and groom were unhappy, but guess who was even more unhappy?

The Italian woman and her daughter who'd just baked for a month and a half! Telling Mom they'd run out of cookies was like telling a Swiss banker he has no idea how much is in his account. My mom knew exactly how much we baked, how much we brought, and she knew someone had taken a bunch! To say she was angry would be the understatement of the century.

I took it as the supreme compliment. If someone was willing to commit larceny for our baking, our cookies must have been fantastic. But since all the Italian women at the wedding knew we'd baked, and our cookies were stolen, our good name was saved and we didn't get thumbs-down. But man, what a disappointment.

I hope the thieves gained twenty pounds. The good news is these little almond cookies are still Donna's favorites.

Buttery Iced Almond Cookies with a Cherry
Makes approximately 36 cookies

They're clearly good enough to steal. There was a cup of finely chopped almonds in Eva's original recipe, which we eliminated, but you don't have to.

INGREDIENTS

1 cup butter

1 cup sugar

2 egg yolks

1 teaspoon almond extract

2 cups flour

1 cup finely chopped almonds (optional)

Maraschino (or Luxardo) cherries, cut into fourths

STEPS

1. Preheat the oven to 325°F. Cream the butter and sugar until light and fluffy.

2. Add the egg yolks and almond extract to the butter and sugar and mix well.

3. Add the flour and optional almonds. Mix thoroughly, or truthfully.

4. Form the dough into 1-inch balls, and place them on an ungreased baking sheet.

5. Flatten balls to ¼ inch thickness with the floured bottom of a flat glass.

6. Bake the cookies for 15 minutes.

7. Frost them with almond-flavored icing (see recipe below) and top with a cherry sliver when cooled.

Almond Frosting:

1 tablespoon butter

1 cup powdered sugar

4 tablespoons whipping cream

½ teaspoon almond flavoring

Dash of salt

STEPS

1. In a medium pot over medium heat, melt the butter and stir in the powdered sugar, cream, almond flavoring, and salt.

2. Whisk the mixture until completely smooth.

3. Frost the almond cookies (and remember to place a cherry on top).

Weeding Out Prospective Suitors

Number two on my mom's priority list was finding suitable mates for her children, which she did not make easy. This was every bit as important as winning on *The Price Is Right*, and maybe more so because grandchildren were on the line.

In ninth grade, I sort of had a boyfriend named Jack. He bought me a chocolate rabbit for Easter. When I showed it to my mom, she said I had to give it back because he would expect something from me. So I hid it under my bed. If the chocolate had been tastier, I would have devoured it instantly. Jack also gave me a ring that turned my finger green, but I loved it. In spite of the fact that I was never allowed to go out with him, I think our romance lasted a whole two months.

When I was a junior in high school, Chuck, who sat in front of me in English class, dared to write me a note professing his like for me. "I dig you, but do you dig me?" was how he so eloquently phrased it. Then he went on to romantically explain that he'd never dated a decent girl, so he wasn't quite sure how to go about it. We decided he'd come over on a Saturday night. I spent the whole day cleaning instead of primping and ended up wearing my hair in a ponytail.

He and I sat next to each other on the living room couch and the TV might have been on. I think my father was in his recliner. My brother Bernie and his wife, who happened to be visiting that day, decided to stick around for the excitement and were in a corner of the living room. My mom was bustling around the kitchen, and my sister may have been there. I've conveniently blocked out most of the evening from my mind.

My mom served delicious apple pie and didn't ask too many questions—very unlike her. Chuck actually stuck around for an hour or two. When he left, I walked him to the door and he got up the nerve to plant a kiss on me that left me woozy at the top of the basement stairs. That's how good it was. I was secretly thankful for those indecent girls who'd been helping him practice.

The next time he showed up, he surprised me on a Saturday night in February, walking three miles to see me. My sister didn't think he should stay because my parents were at church, but it's not like we were alone in my bedroom with me in a negligee.

I don't know why she didn't just say, "Let's make him a cup of tea and he can stay a while since he walked all this way. Mom and Dad will be home soon anyway." We were always so hospitable to everyone except boys who made the mistake of trudging through Pennsylvania in the dead of winter to see me.

"Why does he have to go?" I asked, but I knew my parents would probably blow a gasket. So, instead of fighting her, I sat beside him in the back seat of the car as she drove him home, still shocked that he'd walked all that way in the cold just to see me.

That was the last time he made any attempt to visit. The next time I saw him he was making out with some girl after a basketball game. I'm certain we cured him of ever wanting to date a decent girl again.

Then, in my senior year of high school, I had a crush on a boy who was nice, smart, cute, and funny, who asked me to the Christmas semi-formal. We doubled with a friend and her date. They were in the front seat. As the driver was turning the car around after making a wrong turn, my crush unexpectedly leaned over and gave me a rather wet kiss, something I'd never experienced. My romantic response "Well, that was certainly unexpected" surely cut him off at the knees. The rest of the night lumbered on clumsily. He apologized for the kiss thirty-seven years later in a lovely email, and we both confessed our teenage awkwardness.

In summary, my family made sure I saw zero action in high school. My lack of experience and tact cemented it.

Once I hit college, things improved, but I knew any visiting prospective suitor had to be warned about my family, and my mom in particular. She had a childlike frankness that tended to leave young men stunned. To protect myself, I sat at the dining room table with her laughing way too loud. I thought it would prove to whichever brave fellow she was interrogating that she was kidding (she wasn't). This made me look like a nervous hyena and rarely worked.

If she didn't like him, she'd spend a long time looking at him, focusing specifically on features she didn't like. Sometimes she'd even mention them. The man I eventually married was sitting across from her once and she blurted out, "Roger, ha come you gotta dose lilla white a marks on your teet?" He hadn't thought about the white spots on his teeth in years (thanks, Mom) and explained that they might have been the result of a fever, but he wasn't sure.

Sometimes, after staring at a defect, she'd say things about the young man to me, in Italian, so he couldn't understand. Although my parents purposely didn't teach us Italian, we understood enough to know when someone was being dissed.

It was uncomfortable if she didn't like him, but it was almost worse if she did.

I had a friend, who was a handsome, personable, Italian, Catholic optometrist, who unwittingly visited during the Christmas season. Better than a trifecta, Mom decided he was perfect. So, of course, he was invited to my brother Bernie's house for a Christmastime dinner.

Because he was a "doctor," he got to bypass all qualifying rounds as Mom launched into questions regarding his approximate wealth, then segued into her own health problems, but only after telling him what a wonder I was and that any man who got me would be lucky.

When it was time for dinner, Mom held up her hands and dramatically yelled, *"Wait! Letta da dottor eat first!"* My siblings and sisters-in-law let out a tiny collective gasp followed by quiet chuckles. Even they couldn't believe she would be so bold.

He tried, unsuccessfully, to stifle his smile as she did her best to get everyone to stand behind him at the buffet table. That was the moment I perfected my eye roll.

She begged my brothers to take lots of pictures so she could show him off to her friends, even though our on-again, off-again, long-distance relationship ended up being more friendly than romantic. I decided then I'd never go on a cruise with him and my mom because if the ship went down, it was clear whom she'd save.

We probably have twenty photographs of him with everyone in the family. I couldn't fit them all on one page if I tried. He's even in a shot with my blonde sister-in-law and nephew.

After a while, I just had to laugh. If you're wondering, I'm the dark-haired girl who's forcing a smile in these photos. If Mom could have trapped him in the wine cellar and forced him to marry me, she would have.

But the pinnacle of my embarrassment was yet to come. Rick, the guy who counted religious icons with me, got past her inspections, but not without her telling me in Italian one night (with him sitting right there) that he was nice and she really liked him, but his hair was getting thin and she didn't like his beard, or his pants. Then she said, "Rick, you're a nice-lookin' a boy, ha come you gadda wear dose a baggy pants? You make enough a money, can'd you buy some a nize a pants?"

I forbade her to say anything more. She lasted almost a whole fifteen minutes without a word, but as we were leaving she started pacing and exploded with "Eeeeefa I was a your mother, I would a sneak into your room late at night anna cut off datta damma beard!"

Miraculously, Rick remained my bearded friend. It helped that he was Italian, and had a similar grandmother, so he understood her volatile transitions and found her amusing. Our folks got to know each other, and sometimes he'd visit with his parents.

As a rule, I never left anyone alone with my mother, even for a minute, because . . . well, by now you know why. She once told a woman we'd been friends with for decades that she was absolutely certain a boy who had just walked past was wearing a fake nose. (He wasn't. He was also the woman's son.) We never saw them again.

I'd been friends with Rick for a few years and naively thought she couldn't possibly embarrass me further. We were all sitting at the dining room table, munching salami, bread, and cheese. There was homemade wine, coffee, and a few cookies waiting to be eaten. Our dads were in the garden discussing tomato plants, as Italian men do. I hesitated, but felt fairly confident things were going well, so I left Rick and his mom alone with my mother for a few minutes as I ran to take clothes out of the dryer in the basement.

Less than five minutes later, as I made my way upstairs, past the kitchen and into the dining room, Rick was subtly but frantically motioning that we had to talk privately. As we walked into the hallway, he doubled over in laughter, claiming my mom almost made him pee his pants. I braced myself.

He said that conversation had gotten a little quiet around the table, and my mother, looking to fill the gap and never at a loss for words, said, "Do you know dat inna forty-three years of a marriage Robert has a never seen a me naked?" I sank to my knees moaning, "Nooooooooooo!"

My mother came of age when nice women didn't want to appear as though they'd ever heard of sex, let alone willingly participate in it. Sex was more of a duty back then, like scrubbing filthy socks. So this statement must have felt like a final grasp at dignity for a Catholic woman who'd given birth to five children. Apparently, this was a proclamation Mom made frequently, because our neighbor, Mrs. Smeltzer, confessed she'd heard it too.

Rick said he and his mother paused for a moment, trying hard not to laugh, but wondered what the correct response should be. "What do you say when somebody says that?" he asked while gasping for air through laughter. He said they were both at a loss for words, so they silently nibbled their salami, smiled, and said, "Oh, that's nice."

After they left, my stunned question was "Ma! Why would you tell them that?" Her answer? "Well, ittsa true."

That was the point at which I realized I might be single for a very long time. At least Mom was separating the wheat from the chaff for me.

Pasta with Pesto

Serves 6

This was not a recipe my mom was familiar with, but the first time I made it for her, she said, "Dis issa da best I ever had!" It's easy, delicious, and full of basil and garlic. (I got the recipe from a bag of basil!) Plus, if you're like I was, you won't get to date much, so you may as well enjoy pesto breath!

INGREDIENTS

1 ½ cups basil leaves, lightly packed (stems trimmed off; leaves rinsed and dried)

2 large cloves of garlic

⅓ generous cup pine nuts or walnuts

½ generous cup Parmigiano Reggiano or Romano cheese

⅓ generous cup extra-virgin olive oil

Salt and pepper

1 pound of pasta, preferably rotini or fusilli

STEPS

1. Add 1 teaspoon of salt to a large pot of water, and bring to a boil.

2. In a food processor, add the basil, garlic, and pine nuts. Process until finely chopped.

3. Add the cheese and oil and process 30 seconds to 1 minute, until thoroughly mixed into a creamy pesto spread.

4. Place the pasta into the boiling water and cook until al dente.

5. Reserving 1 cup of hot pasta water, drain the pasta, then place into a large bowl.

6. Add at least half the pesto, and a little of the pasta water, until you have a nice consistency. If you like more pesto, add more along with additional hot water to keep it creamy.

7. Sprinkle with salt and pepper to taste. Garnish with a sprig of basil and serve with grated cheese and some crushed red pepper flakes.

Lemon Ricotta Pound Cake Mouthgasm

Makes 2 medium loaves

Because a *mouthgasm* is as close as you'll probably get if you're a nice Italian Catholic girl.

Pound Cake

INGREDIENTS

1 ½ cups cake flour

2 teaspoons baking powder

1 teaspoon kosher salt

1 ½ sticks softened butter

1 (15 ounces) container of Galbani ricotta cheese

1 ½ cups granulated sugar

3 large eggs

1 teaspoon pure vanilla extract

Zest of 2 lemons

2 tablespoons fresh-squeezed lemon juice

¼ teaspoon lemon oil

Lemon Glaze

INGREDIENTS

1 ½ tablespoons melted butter

1 cup powdered sugar

1 tablespoon lemon juice

1 tablespoon whipping cream

STEPS

1. Preheat the oven to 350°F. Generously grease two small loaf pans, or an 8 x 5-inch loaf pan and an additional 5-inch round but deep casserole dish. (There is too much batter for just one loaf.) I've made this twice and it stuck to the pan both times, so try flouring the pan after greasing it so it doesn't stick.

2. In a medium bowl, combine the flour, baking powder, and salt. Stir to blend and set it aside.

3. Using a mixer, cream the softened butter until smooth, then add the ricotta and granulated sugar until well blended, about 3 minutes.

4. With the machine running, add the eggs, one at a time.

5. Add the vanilla, lemon zest, lemon juice, and lemon oil, until combined.

6. Then add the dry ingredients, a little at a time until combined.

7. Pour the batter into the prepared pans. Do not fill the pans higher than three-quarters full or they might overflow and you don't want to waste this! Bake until a toothpick inserted comes out clean and dry, 45 to 60 minutes, or 30 to 35 minutes for smaller pans.

8. Remove from the pans while warm. When removing from the pans, be sure to run a knife along the edges before you flip the cakes over. Some might stick to the bottom. (Hopefully if you've floured the pan, it won't!)

9. While the pound cake is cooling off, mix the melted butter, powdered sugar, lemon juice, and whipping cream until completely smooth. Drizzle it over the slightly warm loaves. Serve while still warm for a complete *mouthgasm.*

Trudging up the Hill
to Acceptance and Maturity

From birth until I was thirteen, I dined out twice. (I did tour the McDonald's in Beaver Falls with the Girl Scouts and got a hamburger once, so I guess that counts.) OK, three times. I have a vague recollection of eating French fries at a Woolworths with my mom once, but that could have just been a dream.

My father didn't believe in eating out. Even stopping at the local ice-cream place took a fair amount of begging. He'd smoothly drive past whatever restaurant we were begging to go to, and say, "What restaurant? Oh, did you want to stop? Well, too late now. We have better stuff than that at home." This always left me wondering whether he was cheap or we were poorer than I realized.

The first time I ever ate out I was five years old. It was the middle of winter and my mother pulled me out of kindergarten to go to lunch with her and Ethel Bloom, the Stanley Home Products lady. My mother wouldn't pull me out of school even if I was a bloody lump, so I knew this was a big deal.

I was so excited to be going to a restaurant, but was humiliated that my mom made me put on my big puffy leggings in front of the whole class before we left. I knew it would be worth it, though.

In the 1960s, people used to come to your home to sell things. There was Ethel Bloom, our Stanley Home Products lady; the Avon lady; the Fuller Brush man, who always left a tiny bottle of cheap perfume for you; encyclopedia salespeople; vacuum cleaner salesmen; and people who sold pots and pans door-to-door like my brother did for a while. Door-to-door salespeople in the 1960s relied on the fact that most people, when pushed to buy something, get really squirmy and are too nice to say no to your face.

Ethel was taking us to lunch because Mom had apparently achieved a level unsurpassed in Stanley history for buying things like furniture polish, brooms, mops, and scrub brushes. Mom, not only bought them, she held on to her Stanley products for decades. I found a thirty-year-old can of Stanley Furniture Cream under the sink, in the 1980s.

Ethel was a great businesswoman who dressed well, wore bright red lipstick, liked my mom, and could have sold her every home product Stanley ever made. **Correction:** Ethel did sell my mom every home product Stanley ever made. My mother loved Ethel because she was smart, self-sufficient, and probably rich, so it was mutually beneficial.

I sat in the back seat of Ethel's noisy black Volkswagen Beetle, inhaling gas fumes, and didn't care. I couldn't believe that in a few minutes I'd be able to sit down at a table, order whatever I wanted, and they'd bring it.

We went to the Garden Gate Restaurant in Butler, Pennsylvania. It had that single-story, yellow-brick penitentiary look that a lot of places had in the 1950s and '60s. I ordered fried chicken with mashed potatoes, gravy, and my favorite drink, chocolate milk. That lunch confirmed that restaurants were actually heaven.

I was thirteen before I ate out again. We went to the Brown Derby for

Bernie's rehearsal dinner, where I fell in love with baked potatoes with butter and sour cream. My dad complained about the bill for decades because there were sixteen in the bridal party alone, plus family members on both sides.

Things improved dramatically from my teenage years to my twenties, and restaurants were no longer a wonderland for me. But they were still a thrill for my mother, who didn't drive because of a spinout episode when she was learning. She had the whole family in the car, and my dad said, "OK, we're coming to a curve, slow down." She hit the brakes a little too hard and sent the car into a spin, leaving my dad with even less hair. She refused to get behind the wheel after that. Since I knew she rarely got out, I decided to take her to lunch.

After dutifully majoring in elementary education in college to please my parents, I learned there was a glut of teachers. I also found out that educators in western Pennsylvania didn't make enough to live on in 1977. I also discovered (after student teaching) that I hungered to be out in the world, not feeling like I was stuck in a classroom. That led me to take a sales representative job because it offered freedom, a company car, and a $12,000 starting salary, plus bonuses.

It also forced me to spend my days trying to make Listerine, Listermint, Efferdent, Effergrip, Schick Razor Blades, and Sinutabs sound exciting. My territory included my hometown, so after a soul-numbing morning of sales I knew taking Mom to lunch would be a good diversion.

Within two minutes of my arrival, she was ready to go with purse in hand and a huge smile on her face. We drove to Eat'n Park in Beaver Falls and sat in a comfortable booth where Mom read the menu very closely, trying to decide whether to get breakfast or lunch.

The waitress came by and asked if we were ready. Mom had a few questions but seemed ready, so I ordered my usual salad and my mother began:

Mom: "Honey, can a you please a tell a me what's inna dissa salad?"

Waitress: "Well, that's our chef salad with meat and cheese."

Mom: "You ting it's a good?"

Waitress: "Yeah, it's good!"

Mom: "Tell a me, honey, what you ting is a good a here?"

Waitress: "Well, it depends on what you like."

Mom: "How do dey make a da fish?"

Waitress: "Well, they can fry it or broil it."

Mom: "Is itta pretty fresh?"

Waitress: "Yeah, it's fresh."

Mom: "And a, honey, what a kind a meat is inna da chef salad?"

Waitress: "Well, there's ham, plus eggs and cheese in it."

Mom: "How about a you suggest a for a me, honey, 'cause I don'd a know what's a good . . . Frenzy, you ting a I should get a breakfast or lunch?"

Me: "I think you'll like the breakfast."

Mom: "Yeah, I ting a breakfast sounds a pretty good . . . OK, honey, I wanna two eggs, how you say it, Frenzy?"

Me: "Over e—"

Mom (interrupting): "So you can a deep a da bread in dem! And I'll take a da ham, bacon, and a sausage."

Waitress: "Well, you can only get one—ham, bacon, or sausage."

Mom: "Oh, you mean I canna only pick a one?"

Waitress: "Yeah, I'm sorry."

Mom: "OK, den a honey, I ting I'll a take a da bacon. And a,
honey, make a sure da potatoes are crunchy, dats a da
way I like a dem. Honey, can I have another cup a coffee?
Dissa one really hitta da spot."

OK, I know I made the big speech about how, after Mother-Daughter
Night, I had more appreciation for my mom, and was never going to be
embarrassed by her again, but even in my twenties I could feel myself
slipping. I just prayed she wouldn't take out her partial plate and use the
prongs to pick at her remaining teeth right there in the restaurant. She
was famous for that.

Then I looked at her across from me. She smiled and said, "Honey,
dis is a so nice datta you're taking a me out to lunch. I wish a we could a
do it all a da time."

How could I do anything but love this woman, partial plate and all?
I'd wasted all those years being embarrassed by her when I should have
been enjoying her. The waitress even got a kick out of her and we all
ended up laughing.

Mom was helping me trudge up the hill to maturity. So, instead of
trying to correct and change her, I reminded myself to keep smiling and
remember her classic lines. I knew they'd come in handy one day.

Italian Ricotta Cookies—Lemon or Orange

Makes about 50

A sweet way to end even the most embarrassing lunch.

INGREDIENTS

1 ¼ cups sugar

½ cup butter at room temp

1 egg at room temp

¼ teaspoon salt

15 ounces Galbani ricotta at room temp (Galbani is the best; it's never gritty. I've probably said that already!)

½ teaspoon vanilla

Zest of three lemons (I like lemon best, but you can use the zest of 1 large orange instead.)

2½ cups flour

½ teaspoon baking soda

½ teaspoon baking powder

Nonpareils

Icing:

2 cups powdered sugar

2 tablespoons unsalted butter

3 tablespoons whipping cream

3 teaspoons (or more) fresh lemon or orange juice

Pinch of salt

STEPS

1. Preheat the oven to 350°F.

2. In a medium bowl with a mixer, cream the sugar and butter.

3. Add the egg, salt, ricotta, vanilla, and zest.

4. In a separate bowl, sift the flour, baking soda, and baking powder.

5. Add the dry ingredients slowly to the liquid ingredients and mix thoroughly.

6. Drop batter by a tablespoon or small ice-cream scoop onto a cookie sheet.

7. Bake 12 minutes in the oven.

8. While the cookies are baking, in a medium bowl, combine the icing ingredients.

9. Let the cookies cool, then ice and immediately sprinkle with nonpareils.

10. If not serving the cookies in a couple days, don't sprinkle them. The color will run and they won't be pretty.

Say What You Need to Say

I was in a district sales meeting in a Cleveland hotel conference room, watching my boss give what everyone agreed was a brilliant presentation on the wonders of Listerine. He dazzled the crowd with a forty-eight-ounce bottle of Listerine dressed in an adorable little Pittsburgh Steelers outfit.

It was that exact moment I thought to myself, *Dear God, if I have to do this one more day, I will surely die.* I just couldn't get excited about Listerine and something in me wanted to write. I decided I was quitting.

The decision was the easy part. Telling my parents was a skosh more challenging because I'd also decided I was moving to Los Angeles. My great college friend, Rick, lived there. You remember . . . he was the guy who counted religious icons with me, and learned, with his mom, that my dad had never seen my mother naked.

I'd vacationed in LA and it seemed like a cool place to live for a while, plus Rick was my best guy friend and knew a girl who needed a roommate, so I figured, *Why not?* Plus, an ex-boyfriend had just moved into my apartment complex, so I was very ready to leave.

I'd navigated leaving-home issues before and it was never easy. After

I got accepted into college, my brothers had to come in and argue for letting me go (even though school was only an hour and a half away). It took a lot of negotiating, but my parents finally relented. After college, when I landed the sales representative job, it took more convincing to get my parents to agree that having an apartment in Ohio was going to be easier for my commute. (It helped that Bernie and his wife lived there.)

Moving to California was a whole new hurdle. My father accepted it with his usual grace, but thought I was crazy for moving there without a job. (He was right.) My mom agreed with him and took much more convincing because she was adamantly against her Lilla Frenzy moving far away from parents who worked so hard to give her a good life.

Mom and I were in the kitchen talking about my upcoming move. She was mopping the floor, crying, saying, "Why you gadda move a so damn a far away? Why can't you be like a your brothers anna stay here and get married?"

"Because I don't want to stay here and get married."

"But a you have a good a job, makin' a good a money."

"But I hate my job, Ma!"

"Your father was gonna build you a nice a lilla house right beside ours, so you could a be close. You're my lilla gal a—you can't a leave!"

Sometimes genius strikes when you least expect it. I knew there was no way I was going to win this, so I said the words she'd been longing to hear for years: "But, Ma, if I move to Los Angeles, you can visit and finally see *The Price Is Right*!"

It was as if the tears immediately reversed course and backed up into her tear ducts. She stopped mopping, looked up at me beaming, and said, "Really, Frenzy, you ting I have a chance?"

I reassured her, "Of course, you have as good a chance as anybody!"

Hazelnut Thumbprints
with Nutella or Chocolate Ganache

Makes about 36

When guilt over manipulating your mom is just too much, these will get you through.

INGREDIENTS

½ cup packed brown sugar

1 cup butter, softened

1 teaspoon vanilla

2 egg yolks

2 cups unbleached flour

½ teaspoon salt

2 egg whites, slightly beaten

1½ cups finely chopped hazelnuts (I use the dry-roasted ones from Trader Joe's; they're really good.)

Nutella, for the filling, or chocolate ganache (see recipe below)

Powdered sugar, for decoration (optional)

STEPS

1. Preheat the oven to 350°F.

2. In a medium bowl, cream the sugar and butter, then add the vanilla and egg yolks.

3. In a separate bowl, mix the flour and salt.

4. Combine the flour mixture with the butter mixture.

5. Roll the dough into small balls ¾ to 1 inch in diameter.

6. Dip the dough balls into the egg whites, then roll them in the hazelnuts.

7. Place them on a baking sheet and press the centers with your thumb to form an indentation.

8. Bake for 8 minutes.

9. Remove the cookies from the oven, reset the indentation, and bake for 5 more minutes.

10. Remove from the heat.

11. Once they're cooled, drop a teaspoon of Nutella or chocolate ganache into the indentation.

12. Sprinkle them lightly with powdered sugar.

Chocolate Ganache

INGREDIENTS

1 cup Nestle semi-sweet chocolate chips

½ cup whipping cream

STEPS

1. In a small saucepan over low heat, add the chocolate chips and whipping cream and stir with a whisk, until the chips are completely melted and the mixture is smooth.

Da Holy Hour

Rick and I left for LA on a sunny October day in my dad's light-green 1971 Chevy Impala with snow tires and a hundred thousand miles on it. It took us four days to cross the country with only my clothes, toiletries, and Schwinn bike hanging off the back of the trunk. The Chevy was ugly but made it effortlessly. (Side note: The car was so unattractive that even though I'd left the keys in the ignition, in broad daylight in Beverly Hills, it sat untouched.) Eight months later, Mom and Dad made their first visit to Los Angeles. Getting Dad there could be classified a miracle since my father assumed everyone in California was unbalanced.

Rick knew all the quintessential LA places, and we took my parents to each one. There was a gorgeous Spanish-style outdoor restaurant called Lawry's California Center, with fountains and colorful flowers tumbling out of terra-cotta pots everywhere you looked. Lawry's enjoyed perfect Southern California weather, plus wandering mariachi bands and good food. My parents loved it.

We also took them to Disneyland, the Farmers Market—Mom's favorite place, and a very crowded Mexican restaurant at the top of a tall building in Santa Monica, where Rick had to escort Mom outside because she was claustrophobic. As they got out the door, she looked at him very seriously and said, "Oh, thank a you, Reek. I couldn't breathe in dare and iffa you can't breathe, you may as well be dead!"

But the moment Mom had waited for, for years, was finally coming. I had sent for tickets and we were going to be in the studio audience of *The Price Is Right*.

It may have started as a last grasp at the fame she dreamed of as a young woman, or maybe because she thought Bob Barker was cute. But after the card-party incident, Mom was adamant she was getting on that show to prove the woman in her card club wrong for ever doubting her. Never underestimate a Neapolitan's finely honed revenge gene.

We drove to CBS Studios beside the Original Farmers Market on Fairfax and Third. I parked the Chevy and we got in line. While in line, we were given name tags to put on.

As we waited, Mom was like a little kid. Grabbing my arm every few minutes, she said, "Frenzy, you think a dey call onna me?" Then looking heavenward, she said, "Jesus, please if a dey call on me, tella me what a to say. Frenzy, what if I get a tongue a tied? Jesus, please, you put a da words in a my mouth . . . OK?"

Jesus and I had our hands full that morning with questions and requests. My dad trailed behind us muttering, "What are you so excited for? It's only a stupid TV show."

We stood in line, name tags on, waiting to be interviewed by the show's producer. He was a dark-haired man in his thirties, whose shirt strained to stay buttoned around his middle. My mother was interviewed first. If she'd been any more excited, she would have experienced liftoff. She knew this was her time to shine.

Producer: "Hello, Mary, why don't you tell me a little bit about yourself?"

Mom: "Well, a every day at a eleven a clock, I gatta go to da TV
and a put on a Bob a Barker anna da *Price Is a Right* a.
My husband calls itta da holy hour. I just a love a his
show and a I think he's a very nize a man."

She smiled her biggest smile and was happier and peppier than I'd ever seen her. This was as close as she'd ever come to her dream of stardom, right up there with the time she won for Prettiest Brunette and Miss Beaver County.

I was terrified they wouldn't pick her. I worried, *What if her accent was too hard to understand? What if she was too old, too excited, or too heavy?* I didn't want to see her heartbroken if she wasn't chosen.

The producer then interviewed my dad and me, both dull as nasal spray compared to Mom. They showed us into the air-conditioned studio and seated us in one of the last rows in the back. Mom was convinced this was a bad sign.

The corners of her smile drooped. She leaned toward me, and in a lifeless voice she murmured, "I don't a think a they gonna pick us if a they put us all a da way inna da back, Frenzy." I didn't want to get her hopes up, but I also didn't want to even contemplate her disappointment if she wasn't picked for the show of her dreams, so I borrowed one of my parents' favorite phrases in times of stress: "Well, we'll see."

Loud, upbeat music was playing to get the crowd excited. My mother was clapping her hands, offbeat as usual. No matter what the song, she always clapped the same beat. And on this day, she didn't care, she just wanted to make sure she looked enthusiastic so the producers and directors onstage could see she was the right choice.

This further embarrassed my father, who had the same look on his face he sported while waiting for a doctor's appointment. "Keep quiet," he kept saying. "You always gotta make a show, don't you?"

"I don'd a care, I'm a here to have a gooda time and I'm a gonna have a gooda time!" she said defiantly with a firm nod of her head.

I sat between the two of them, wondering how I was going to get through the next hour, let alone deal with her if she wasn't picked. It was just too much to consider, so I started clapping my hands and looking excited too, thinking if they didn't pick her, they might pick me. That, she could handle.

Bob's announcer, Johnny Olson, came into the audience, flirting with all the women, and gave me what my mouthwash background told me was a Scope-laced kiss on the mouth. Mom was convinced this was a sign I was definitely going to be a contestant. I chalked it up to men being men.

"You're a young a gal . . . What do dey wand wit an old a baddle-axe a like a me? Dey gonna peek a you, honey," she said, smiling weakly and trying to hide her disappointment.

The audience lights went down and out came Bob Barker, dressed handsomely in a dark suit, the ultimate game show host. He told a funny story, then got down to business, asking Johnny Olson to announce the first four contestants.

My mother wasn't one of them. My insides began to tighten. *Oh no,* I thought, *I brought them all the way out here and now she only has a few chances left to be chosen. What if she doesn't make it? Please let her make it,* I prayed, and began wondering what I'd have to promise God to swing a deal. I'd forgotten the heavy hitter was right beside me.

If you're not familiar with the mysteries of Catholicism, there's a prayer Catholics save for things like the World Series and childbirth. Remember the stack of novena prayers Mom had at the sewing machine shrine to Jesus? And remember that you pray the novena for nine straight days, and at the end you're supposed to miraculously get what you prayed for?

My mother, who never went a day without at least seven holy medals pinned to her bra, had made about nine billion novenas in her lifetime. Finally, someone was listening, because the second round of contestants was called, and Johnny Olson said, "Mary Tunno (Ton-o), come on down!" The pronunciation was unfortunate, but my mother never noticed. Her big moment finally came and she was ready. She knew this was her time to shine.

"Meeeeee! Dey peeked a me!" she squealed as she rose from her seat. She trotted down the aisle in her bright blue dress, waving her fists triumphantly, radiantly flashing her Miss Beaver County smile, ready to meet her idol, Bob Barker.

My father was gobsmacked. He couldn't believe that she said she'd get picked and then got picked. I imagined everyone in our small town, including the woman from Mom's card club, thinking the same thing.

She'd barely reached the microphone on Contestants' Row when I had that familiar feeling of unease because she wasn't just in front of friends, she was on national television. Anything could happen. Mom barely remembered where she was from, but that didn't stop her from immediately launching into her version of how she got to the show.

Mom (nervous and almost tearful): "I been a wanting a to see you for a long a time a."

Bob: "Well, Mary, all you had to do was turn on your television."

(Mom smiles tenderly, completely charmed by her hero.)

Bob: "Where do you live?"

Mom (still nervous, forgets her hometown): "In Pennsylvania."

Bob: "Oh, so you're out here on vacation."

Mom: "Well yes (she becomes very animated), I came a because a my daughter, she says 'Ma, you wanna see Bob a Barker? I'm a gonna move to California and you getta to come here.'"

Bob: "Your daughter moved to California, just so you could come and see me?"

Mom: "It's a God's a true."

Bob: "Now, Mary, she didn't move out here, so you could come and see me."

Mom: "She did!"

Bob: "She did?"

Mom turns and points to me and says, "She's a back a dare."

Bob: "Where's the daughter? Stand up, will you?"

Oh God, I thought, *here we go.* I slowly stand to applause from the crowd, about to die, not from the usual embarrassment, but from new, even worse, nationally televised embarrassment.

Bob: "Did you really move to California just so Mary could visit you and see me?"

This was one of those dangerous times when silence was probably the best course of action. So I smiled, tilted my head, opened my mouth, and looked as though I was about to speak when Bob interjected and said, "That's all I needed to know."

Mom (not giving up without a fight): "Please a Bob."

Bob (chiding her): "Mary."

Mom: "Believe a me, it's a God's a true!"

Bob: "What'd you say?"

Mom: "It's a God's a true!"

Bob: "Now, Mary."

Mom: I wouldn't a lie to you, Bob. **She had a good a job!"** (She almost loses it and actually starts to raise her voice at Bob, but checks herself just in time.)

Bob: "She gave up a good job?"

Mom (much more meekly): "Dat's a rite a."

Bob: "Now she's out here on welfare, just so you could be on the show?"

The camera pans up to me and I nod with a smile. What else was there to do?

Bob: "You know what's the matter here? You know what's the matter? She thinks she's on *Queen for a Day*! That's what's the matter."

Queen for a Day was a daytime TV show that aired from 1956 to 1964, where the woman with the absolute worst life was chosen as queen for a day from a group of four women with equally miserable lives. The studio audience decided the winner with their applause.

Generally, the woman with the most horrifyingly awful existence got the loudest applause and won. Then she was crowned Queen for a Day, draped in a red cape with ermine trim, given roses, and got to walk along a walkway as "Pomp and Circumstance" played. The audience cheered and countless women watching at home wept. (If you ever want to feel better about your life, that's the rerun to watch.)

At this, my mother laughed at Bob and herself, realizing he had her number. But she never let go of her story. I'm sure she thought that if she could just get her daughter's face on TV, along with a good story, she was certain some Hollywood producer would cast me as their next big star. If she couldn't be the star, maybe I could. Unbelievably, the calls never poured in. But my mother was a woman who knew how to milk a moment for all the drama possible.

After that, she forgot her hometown again and was pretty nervous. After several attempts, she correctly estimated the price of a set of luggage and got to leave Contestants' Row and join Bob onstage. She'd come a long way from calling out a number in school and being laughed at by pipsqueaks. As Mom walked onstage and placed a loving kiss on Bob's cheek, I envisioned the card-club lady's enormous plate of steaming-hot crow.

Mom lost another round of price-guessing in the Hi-Lo game. Bob and the audience really tried hard to help her because she wasn't quite sure about the game and was completely unnerved. Bob kept telling the audience to yell louder because my mom couldn't hear what products they were telling her to pick.

She lost that game and I thought she was finished, but she ended up being one of several contestants who got to roll the big wheel in the Showcase Showdown, the grand finale of *The Price Is Right* where the big prizes are given. She rolled the giant wheel and scored a forty-five, then rolled again and got a fifty, totaling ninety-five, almost the highest number possible. That made her one of the two remaining contestants. (More proof that perhaps Saint Anthony was spinning the wheel with her.)

My dad and I sat there incredulous that my mom made it as one of the two finalists! The other contestant was a sweetheart of a woman from Fort Dodge, Iowa, named Darlene Allard.

Mom made a bid on a package that included a dining room set, a bar, and several other items. I didn't think her bid was close enough. She looked up at me hopefully from the stage, but I had a doubtful look on my face. Her hopeful look instantly deflated.

And then it was Darlene's turn. Here's the part that further bolsters my novena theory: Darlene made her first bid, then looked at the screaming crowd, got scared, and nervously changed her bid. The only thing that disqualifies you in this part of the show is overbidding, which is what Darlene did by changing her bid. She then gave my mother the most gracious, loving hug.

So, my mom, with her second-grade education and Italian accent, not only got on the show, got to meet and kiss Bob Barker, but ended up the winner of the showcase.

Final score:

Novena lovers: 1

Nonbelievers: 0

My dad and I looked at each other in shock as we walked down to the stage to greet Mom and Bob Barker. As Mom predicted, he was very sweet. She ended up bringing home:

An elegant dining room set by Broyhill

A handsome set of luggage on wheels by Skyway

A set of Queen Anne dinnerware by Wilton Armetale

A complete service for twelve of gold-plated flatware with chest

A tasteful and elegant walnut bar with three barstools

Thirty square yards of carpeting from West Point–Pepperell

And a delicious serving of crow for the woman in her card club

Best of all, when she got back to New Brighton, she was a celebrity with her *Price Is Right* story in the *Beaver County Times*. But once again, they mangled her name, so she wrote it in on the article she'd cut out and taped together.

Nevertheless, Mom was thoroughly delighted. My best friend Carolyn made a banner congratulating her on being the winner and brought it to my parents' house. The family took photos, holding it in front of the garage. She said being on that show and winning was the best moment of her life. I was thrilled to have played a tiny part in it.

It was another humbling Girls Athletic Association pizza moment. I sat in that crowd and really thought my mom was out of the running after the Hi-Lo contest, and then she rolled almost the highest number you can and was one of the two finalists. This college graduate thought the woman with the second-grade education had missed her bid because her numbers were off. She did not. I used to shake my head at her absolute conviction that she was a winner. And then she won. Maybe I should try to find her old "workout" books and start playing those numbers.

In my teen years, I was always so afraid people would assume I was just like her, associating her lack of education and thick accent with being less than. I've come full circle to say the highest compliment anyone could pay me now would be to say, "Wow, she's just like her mom."

For my mother, not being valued by her parents made her stronger and even more determined to show them and everyone that she was someone. It would have been so easy to slide into resentment and anger, yet she chose to stay positive and never treat her children as she was treated. I'm tremendously thankful for the strength that must have taken.

Her win gave me new respect for people with a vision. I believe there's a reason you're given a dream. The universe, God, whatever you want to call it, wants you to pursue it. And, if you do, things will come together to make it happen. She showed me that if you want something badly enough, you have to go for it. If you think you can do it, you can. You can't listen to people who say you don't have a chance; they're probably just afraid to dream big themselves.

It's been more than four decades since my mother's fifteen minutes of fame, but each year on September 24, the month and day her episode aired, I view that grainy videotape and smile. I do it to honor her and every big dreamer out there. Keep the faith, and keep trying. You never know what life has waiting for you.

Prizewinning Danish Pastry Puffs

Makes about 20 (1 ½ inch) slices

This story deserves a prizewinning recipe. This one (featured in Bernie's Top Fork column in the Youngstown *Vindicator* in the 1980s) was handed down from Bernie's former neighbor Martha May in Canfield, Ohio. She got it from her eighth-grade home economics teacher Wealthie Crawford. Wealthie entered it into a national Bake-Off contest decades ago and won a prize. It is buttery deliciousness!

Crust

INGREDIENTS

½ cup butter, softened

1 cup flour

3 tablespoons cold water

Topping:

½ cup butter

1 cup water

1 teaspoon almond extract

1 teaspoon vanilla extract

1 cup flour

3 large (or extra-large) eggs

STEPS

1. Preheat the oven to 350°F.

2. **For the crust:** In a medium bowl, mix the butter, flour and cold water.

3. Spread the dough into two rectangles (or hearts) on an ungreased cookie sheet.

4. **For the topping:** In a medium-size saucepan, heat the butter and water and bring to a boil so the butter melts.

5. Add the almond extract and vanilla. Then remove from the heat and add the flour immediately.

6. Beat the mixture by hand until smooth, then add the eggs, one at a time, and mix until smooth and thoroughly incorporated.

7. Spread the topping evenly over the crusts and bake in the oven for 45 to 60 minutes, or until golden brown. Let cool.

Icing

INGREDIENTS

2 tablespoons butter

2 cups powdered sugar

1 teaspoon (or more) vanilla

8 tablespoons half-and-half or whipping cream (or more for desired spreading consistency)

Dash or two of salt

STEPS

1. In a saucepan over medium heat, melt the butter and add the powdered sugar, vanilla, half-and-half, and salt.

2. Beat with a whisk until smooth and pourable. (Cream cheese frosting is great on these too!) Pour the icing over the cooled puffs and sprinkle with sliced almonds or chopped walnuts.

A Finely Honed Revenge Gene

In the years after she won, my mother never forgot Bob Barker. She was convinced she'd won because Bob wanted her to have all the prizes. And Bob did give her a fair amount of help by urging the crowd to yell louder, so God bless him.

Naturally, when my father tried to talk Mom into taking the money instead of the prizes, she was adamant they were gifts from Bob and she wanted them in her house even if they didn't fit.

She sent Bob gift packages of nuts and cheese from the Swiss Colony each Christmas to show her appreciation and always got a note of thanks. One year she didn't get an acknowledgment, so she called *The Price Is Right* office. (Only God and some poor, distraught phone operator know how she got that number.) She was told that perhaps the gift had been lost or stolen, but the woman on the phone reassured her that Bob thanked her just the same.

A few days later she received one of her most prized possessions, a personal note from Bob Barker and an 8 x 10 glossy. (Wondering if the letter was really handwritten, we wet the ink and it ran.) We couldn't believe he'd write a personal letter! This was confirmed later by a lovely personal note I received from Bob with the exact same handwriting, after my story of Mom's victory, "Da Holy Hour," ran in the *LA Times* in 2003. She kept the letter in one of her many important-papers purses and put the photo in a double 8 x 10 frame.

One side of the frame held a shot of my brothers running in Pittsburgh's Great Race and the other held Bob Barker's headshot. As far as my mother was concerned, Bob was now family. Bob and my brothers nestled on a doily on top of the stereo near the front door of my parents' home until my mother passed away.

Within days of my mother's passing, I was shocked to find my father with Bob's photo in hand, standing at the trash can. He was tearing up Bob's picture and tossing it in the trash with a satisfied look on his face. Mom always said he was jealous.

But for thirty-one years, my father lived with two dining room sets, a bar in his crowded living room, gold-plated flatware that had lost most of its sheen, luggage, carpeting, and pewter plates they never used. I'm sure he believed Mom would haunt him if he ever tried to get rid of any of it.

Mom left us when she was seventy-eight years old, but twenty years later I found a secret copy of Bob's photo hidden in a manila envelope at the bottom of her *Price Is Right* dining room hutch. In spite of my father's actions, Bob Barker was still in the house. Let me repeat, death cannot weaken a Neapolitan's finely honed revenge gene.

The Best Banana Bread with Chocolate Chips
Makes 2 medium loaves

Revenge is best with moist banana bread and melty chocolate chips. This is one of my most requested recipes, adapted from the Kona Inn Banana Bread Recipe. My mom first added chocolate chips to her banana bread recipe in the 1960s, and I can't imagine it any other way.

INGREDIENTS

2 cups flour

1 teaspoon salt

2 teaspoons baking soda

1 cup butter, softened

2 cups sugar

2 cups mashed ripe banana (about 6 medium)

4 eggs, slightly beaten

1 cup walnuts, chopped

1 cup chocolate chips (optional: but trust me, utterly fantastic, especially when the bread is warm!)

STEPS

1. Preheat the oven to 350°F.

2. In a medium bowl, stir together the flour, salt, and baking soda.

3. In a separate large bowl, mix the butter, sugar, banana, eggs, walnuts, and chocolate chips, if using.

4. Add the dry ingredients and stir until the batter is thoroughly blended.

5. Pour the batter into two greased and floured (9 x 5-inch) loaf pans (you might have some left over and can put it in a few paper-lined cupcake tins).

6. Bake in the oven until a toothpick inserted in the center comes out clean, about 65 minutes.

7. Start checking for doneness after about 45 minutes (especially if the muffins are in with the rest; they will cook quickly, so check them after 20 minutes). And don't worry, this bread will look dark but is delicious.

8. To keep it moist, butter the top thoroughly while it's hot, then remove it from the pan, and immediately place it in foil or plastic wrap.

A Pooty Butterfly—Mom Returns

One of my prized possessions is a beautiful coverlet my mother crocheted with butterflies and flowers all over it. She loved butterflies and could magically get them to land on her hand or shoulder.

Mom repeated again and again that after she died she was going to come back as a pooty butterfly. My brother Bernie laughingly shot back with "Yeah, you'll be the biggest damn butterfly around." My mother laughed and smacked him on the head.

Well, the biggest damn butterfly actually did visit me one evening, maybe seven years after her death. We'd finished a wonderful slow-cooked chuck roast dinner and were taking care of household chores. I was in the cottage home my husband and I lived in, in Glendale, California, when I opened the screen door to my bedroom and stepped out to get something in the laundry. It was dusk, but in flapped the biggest swallowtail butterfly I'd ever seen. I was stunned.

I thought it was doubly strange to see a butterfly that huge and that late in the evening. I yelled, "Oh my God, you guys, come here. My mom's here!" My son and husband came in and we all took turns looking at the giant butterfly that had landed on the wall and wouldn't leave. I excitedly blurted out, "It's my mom . . . Oh my God, she's here!"

My husband decided it wasn't my mom, and even if it was, he didn't want her on the wall of our bedroom. So he took a newspaper and brushed her off the wall and out the door to the back porch. I was not happy because I wanted to keep her on the wall as long as she wanted to stay.

I went to bed that night marveling at the coincidence of it all. When I got up in the morning, I went to the back porch just outside my bedroom on my way to finish more laundry. I was amazed to see my mom butterfly sitting on our patio dining table, as if she was waiting for me (or breakfast).

I was stunned and went to look at her closer. I excitedly yelled to my husband that the butterfly was still here. (Duh . . . you'd think I would have learned.) He came out with the newspaper and scooped her away again. (There's a reason we got divorced.) She fluttered away toward the backyard, but she was large and having a hard time gaining altitude. Our brown Lab saw this moment to take advantage and leaped up and gobbled her in one bite. I was crushed that she was gone, but it all made sense to me.

She kept her promise and really did come back, specifically flapping in to see me. Plus, if I was looking for another sign that I needed a divorce, the butterfly moment provided one. And she would never leave without feeding someone, which she did.

When I got to work later that morning, I looked up "giant butterfly" on the internet and the first thing that came up was a photo that looked just like my mom butterfly. It's called a giant swallowtail and has a wingspan of 5.5 to 6.9 inches wide for females and 5.8 to 7.4 for males. And they're found in Southern California. I know this sounds a little woo-woo, but I really think it was her.

Slow-Cooked Chuck Roast
with Onions and Red Wine

Serves 6 to 8

A combo recipe of mine and Mom's that leaves hours for butter-fly-watching.

INGREDIENTS

1 (3 pounds) boneless chuck roast

Meat tenderizer

2 cloves garlic, crushed

1 tablespoon olive oil

½ cup flour for dredging

⅓ bottle of good-quality cabernet or merlot

5 medium red onions, sliced

STEPS

1. Preheat the oven to 350°F. Remove the meat from its pack-aging, rinse it with cold water, and pat to remove excess water.

2. Sprinkle it with meat tenderizer and poke all over with a fork.

3. In a heavy frying pan or cast-iron skillet over medium heat, add the olive oil and garlic.

4. In a large flat dish, add the flour. Dredge the meat in the flour on both sides while heating the garlic and olive oil.

5. Place the meat into the pan with the garlic and brown on both sides.

6. Spray a 13 x 9-inch roasting pan with nonstick spray or oil.

7. Remove the meat and garlic from the frying pan and place into the roasting pan.

8. While the frying pan is still hot, add the wine and deglaze it, scraping up all the remaining flour and garlic.

9. Turn off the heat and set the pan with the wine aside.

10. Lay the onion slices over the beef.

11. Add the wine from the pan to the onions and meat.

12. Cover the pan with aluminum foil and bake for 3 hours or more, until the meat is fork-tender, turning at least once while cooking.

Grab That Embarrassment and Run with It!

My mom would be thrilled that you've read this book about her all the way to the end. I've had a lot of fun at her expense. If she was here, she'd be chasing me with her metal spoon with the gnarled, melted handle. But I inherited my parents' sense of humor and teasing is how our family always showed our love for each other. Well, that and food, of course.

I know my mom's energy is out in the universe somewhere alongside my dad's. I couldn't be prouder to have had them for parents. They taught me what you need to succeed in life: hard work, a sense of humor, and a dream to pursue. I also learned not to waste time being embarrassed about what makes you different, but to grab hold of it and run with it because it's definitely what makes you interesting.

I once read a quote from a brilliant person whose name I don't recall, who said, "The key to life is to take what made you weird as a kid and get people to pay you money for it when you grow up." If anyone other than my siblings and kids buy this book, it's proof that quote is absolutely true and that ham and smart-ass skills do finally pay off.

And I've learned that being embarrassed by your mother comes full circle to haunt you once you become a mother. When my daughter was in kindergarten, I put my ham skills to work for Let's Read a Book Day. I dressed up as Miss Viola Swamp, the mean alter ego of the sweet, but ineffectual schoolteacher, Miss Nelson, in *Miss Nelson is Missing*. I'd painted red circles on my cheeks, dressed in black, and did my best to look as witchlike as possible.

When the classroom door opened, I saw my daughter's eyes open wide with shock and immediate embarrassment. She heard the kids around her laughing and turned slowly to see their smiles. They knew it would be a fun day. Seeing her classmates enjoying me, I saw her do a calming exhale and give me a little smile. I knew she was OK. But, for a few seconds, I felt what my mom must have felt from me for years. I'm sorry, Mom.

Now I leave you with some of my mother's most consistent advice and famous sayings when we were growing up:

> *"Be always nice, have a respect, and a remember,*
> *de appearanze is 100 percent."*
>
> *"You can do anyting a you putta your mind to."*
>
> *"God helps a da one who helps himself."*
>
> *"Columbus took a chanze."*

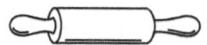

Cherry Cranberry Pie

Serves 8

My mom put together many uncooked pies in the freezer to be baked and eaten later. "Cheery Pay" (cherry pie) was the label written on a ripped piece of paper towel on one of the last pies we found in her freezer after she passed away. So it's appropriate that this recipe for Cherry Cranberry Pie comes at the end of the book. I found this recipe in a Pillsbury ad, and it's great at Christmas. It's sweet, tart, and delicious with vanilla ice cream.

INGREDIENTS

2 Mary Tunno pie crusts

Cherry Cranberry Filling
(see recipe below)

1 tablespoon half-and-half

Mary Tunno Pie Crust

2½ cups flour

1 teaspoon salt

1 tablespoon sugar

1 cup butter, cut into ½-inch pieces

½ cup (or more) ice-cold whole or 2% milk

STEPS

1. In a food processor, combine the flour, salt, and sugar.

2. Add the butter and process until it looks like pea-sized crumbs.

3. Add the milk and pulse until it just comes together.

4. Dump the dough on a lightly floured countertop and squeeze together.

5. Roll the dough out until it's about 1 inch thick, cut it in half, and put one piece on top of the other.

6. Then roll that out to about 1 inch thickness and cut it again, then place one piece on top of the other.

7. Press the layers together and roll it out slightly.

8. Cut it into four pieces, wrap them each in cellophane, and chill until ready to make the pie. (You only need two crusts for this pie.)

9. Freeze the rest until you're ready to use them at a later date. (Be careful if you defrost them in the microwave because they defrost in seconds!)

Cherry Cranberry Filling

1 (21 ounces) can of Comstock More Fruit Cherry Pie Filling

12 ounces fresh or frozen cranberries, rinsed

¾ cup sugar

2 tablespoons cornstarch

STEPS

1. Preheat the oven to 425°F. Roll out one of the dough pieces to about ⅛ inch thickness and wide enough to fit your pie pan with about an inch overhang on all sides.

2. Place the dough into the pie pan.

3. In a medium bowl, combine the cherry cranberry filling ingredients. Fill the pie pan with the filling.

4. Roll out another of the pie-crust pieces to ⅛ inch thickness to cover the pie filling.

5. You can either use a full top crust or slice the dough into strips and weave it like a lattice on top of the pie.

6. Fold the bottom edge of the crust over the top and crimp the edges.

7. If using a whole top crust, poke 10 to 15 holes in the top crust with a fork or knife.

8. Lightly brush the crust with the half-and-half.

9. Bake in the oven for 15 minutes.

10. Then be sure to reduce heat to 350 and bake another 45 minutes, or until the filling starts to bubble. *Buon appetito!*

Acknowledgments

When a book takes forty years to put out there, you can bet a lot of people were involved in very slowly moving it forward. First, let me thank my family: My children, Brandon Jacobs, his wife Ingrid, and their kids Esther and Otto, as well as Anderson Mills and Milena Mills. They've all heard me tell these stories many times and never rolled their eyes. (Clearly, you're not smart-asses like I was.) And thanks to my ex-husband, Roger, who took many of the photos, which helped me remember moments that might have otherwise slipped away.

Thanks to my long-suffering siblings, Bernie and Donna Tunno, Bob and Patty Tunno, and Mary Tunno, who've tolerated me putting them out there with my stories. Thanks also to my nephews and their families: The late Marc Tunno and his kids, Dominic and Julie; Matt and Elissa Tunno and their kids, Nate and Muiriel; Chris Tunno; and Dr. Patrick Tunno and his son, Alessandro.

I also want to thank my cousin Rich Tunno and his wife, Cheri. Cheri was the first one to suggest I write a book because I had so many funny Mom stories, so blame her for this. Thanks to my cousin Nancy, who's had to listen to a great many of these stories over and over and helped me recollect memories. And a loving thank-you to Uncle Richard and Aunt Blanche, undoubtedly in heaven, eating salami sandwiches with my parents. You were like a second dad and mom to me.

I also thank my cousins: Linda, Colleen, Jim, and Gigi for sharing their stories about my mom's parents, who were kind and loving to them. Thanks, Jim, for tracking down documents for me that helped with dates of comings and goings. Thanks to my cousin Cindy for sharing her memories, and I send my gratitude to all my cousins on my mom's side for kindly supporting me in retelling these stories. I hope they haven't offended you. They were my mother's truth. I also thank my family on my dad's side, both here and in Italy, for your kindness, for reading my blog and encouraging me.

It takes a ton of support to keep working on something when you're filled with self-doubt, which is why I want to thank the following people:

Appreciation to Pax Quigley, who taught the first creative-writing class I took at UCLA, when I was convinced I was a terrible writer. She encouraged me to write what I know and thought I was good and my stories were funny. Your encouragement gave me the impetus to continue. And thank you Don Ray, another UCLA teacher who encouraged me from day one and loved my mom stories.

Now on to my many helpful friends: Thanks to Dawn Wilkins and Carolyn Riley, my two besties in the world. You both have read these stories more times than I care to admit, and Dawn, of HelioGraphics.com, you put in many hours of beautiful creative work on this because you are a fabulous, supportive friend. I cannot thank you enough. And thanks to the late but lovely Mrs. R., my surrogate mom—who did not roast goat heads.

Gratitude to Linda Friday, my wonderful friend and graphic artist who created my website and has guided me in so many ways through this mess called life.

Zoe Walrond, thanks for your reading, reviewing, and encouraging me to continue with my stories and blog, and for putting me up when

I'm in LA. Thanks also to lifelong friend and fellow Italian Malina Trozzo, who's had to hear these stories over and over. Thank you, Rick DeLoia. If you hadn't moved to California, I would have never moved and Mom wouldn't have had her dream come true. Thanks also to good friends Mandy Gustafsen, Cynthia Kesselman Nicol Zanzarella, Michael Ehrenberg, Marianna Clarizio, Maria Iezza, Denise Fondo, Chuck Burkett, Anna Taylor, and Myah Hunt, who have followed my blog and read and listened to my stories ad nauseum.

Thanks to Jeff Guillot of Lucent Audio, his graphic designer wife Jen, and his wonderful director, Danielle Quisenberry-Ruvolo, who helped me record the audiobook. Thanks also to Debra Deyan, of Deyan Audio, and her late husband, Bob, who, on his deathbed beckoned me close and whispered, "Fran, finish the f#!cking book." Thanks, Bob and Deb, for giving me my first job as an audiobook narrator and for your friendship and support.

Thanks to Marion Roach Smith, whose blogs on memoir writing were helpful and to her editor, Jill Smolowe, whose editing and review of my book gave me the confidence to proceed with publishing. Thanks to Noah Michelson of the *HuffPost* and to Martin J. Smith, formerly of the *Los Angeles Times Magazine*, both of whom published my essays on Mom winning on *The Price Is Right*. Thanks to Reedsy for connecting me with copy editor Carrie Wicks, whose attention to detail is impressive. Also, thanks to editor Susannah Noel, who was incredibly encouraging and other helpful editors including: Margaret Diehl, Doug Moser, Jodie Fodor, Mark Malatesta, and Laura Fraser.

Thanks also to Milena Mills, who designed my book cover (with input from brother, Brandon Jacobs), and to Karen Minster for her design work on the PDF for the audiobook.

And thanks to all my blog followers including Bernie and Donna's friends, Bob and Patty's friends, Mary's friends, and all my former coworkers, my former radio listeners, my former PTA pals and teachers, my former Stepping Stone Players members, my yoga pals, and so many others. My life has been rich with great friends and followers, and I am so thankful for each of you.

Finally, I want to give a late but heartfelt thank-you to my dad's mom, Maria Giovanna Equizi, who stayed in Italy, raised the kids, cooked, cleaned, ran the farm, and never complained while my grandfather worked in the US for five years to get his citizenship. You both sacrificed so much. Also, thank you to my mom's grandmother, Maria Louisa Carcaise, for loving my mom the way a child should be loved. You made a difference.

About the Author

Fran Tunno lives in Pittsburgh where she enjoys writing, cooking, sharing stories on her blog, and feeding people. Fran's essays have appeared in *The Huffington Post*, the *Los Angeles Times* and *The Pittsburgh Post-Gazette*. She's been featured on NPR's *Snap Judgment* and WritersRead.org. Connect with her on her blog, AtFransTable.com, or at FranTunno.com, especially if you have spatula-wielding mom stories or a great recipe to share!